Language Planning and Student Experiences

Intention, Rhetoric and Implementation

Joseph Lo Bianco and Renata Aliani

MULTILINGUAL MATTERS
Bristol • Buffalo • Toronto

Library of Congress Cataloging in Publication Data
A catalog record for this book is available from the Library of Congress.
Lo Bianco, Joseph.
Language Planning and Student Experiences: Intention, Rhetoric and Implementation /Joseph
Lo Bianco and Renata Aliani.
Bilingual Education and Bilingualism: 93
Includes bibliographical references and index.
1. Language planning. 2. Education, Bilingual. 3. Language policy. 4. Literacy--Government
policy. 5. Bilingualism. 6. Linguistic minorities. I. Title.
P40.5.L35.L6 2013
306.44'9–dc23 2013011926

British Library Cataloguing in Publication Data
A catalogue entry for this book is available from the British Library.

ISBN-13: 978-1-78309-004-4 (hbk)
ISBN-13: 978-1-78309-003-7 (pbk)

Multilingual Matters
UK: St Nicholas House, 31-34 High Street, Bristol BS1 2AW, UK.
USA: UTP, 2250 Military Road, Tonawanda, NY 14150, USA.
Canada: UTP, 5201 Dufferin Street, North York, Ontario M3H 5T8, Canada.

The policy of Multilingual Matters/Channel View Publications is to use papers that are
natural, renewable and recyclable products, made from wood grown in sustainable forests. In
the manufacturing process of our books, and to further support our policy, preference is given
to printers that have FSC and PEFC Chain of Custody certification. The FSC and/or PEFC logos
will appear on those books where full certification has been granted to the printer concerned.

Typeset by R.J. Footring Ltd, Derby
Printed and bound in Great Britain by Short Run Press Ltd

Contents

Figures

Tables

Aims, Limitations and Questions

This volume combines data from ethnographic research in schools with analysis of policy. The focus of the school data is restricted to the last five years, while the policy analysis refers to a much longer period. The research is both longitudinal and intensive, diachronically seeing how languages and language education have been constituted over time in the public consciousness and also synchronically looking at the implementation of language programmes in schools as experienced by relevant parties, especially students. The research introduces methods of data gathering unfamiliar to the field of language policy analysis, especially Q-methodology (Watts & Stenner, 2012; McKeown & Thomas, 1988; Brown, 1993), selected because it complements conventional approaches. The aim is to make a contribution to language planning theory, especially to theory about the implementation of language education policy, called *acquisition planning* by Robert Cooper (1989). Cooper's volume entitled *Language Planning and Social Change* is presented as a kind of career reflection on the 'state of the art' of language planning after its initial decades, from its conception to its emergence as a fully fledged field of academic enquiry. Cooper's volume finishes with the question: 'Is a theory of language planning possible?' He concludes that 'to plan language is to plan society. A satisfactory theory of language planning, therefore, awaits a satisfactory theory of social change' (1989: 182). Whether this is defeatism, pessimism, realism or simply a courteous check against excessive optimism depends on the confidence of the reader in depictions of society, its reproduction and change, but it is likely that any advance to talking more coherently about the relationships between planned language change and social change requires attention at both macro and micro levels.

The language policies of successive Australian governments are a good case study for looking at links between social change and language. Australia has issued a stream of language policies since the 1970s. That a steadfastly monolingual society using the world's dominant auxiliary language should engage so robustly with language policy implies something about shifting social and ideological circumstances. Several of Australia's many language policies have espoused significant and occasionally even radical ambitions for social change. In this way, language planning has been in the service of new visions of the national society, or has fostered new dimensions of national identity, or has anticipated or tried to engineer a new role and presence for citizens in the external world. So strong have these social desires been that these policies can appear to be totally divorced from the mundane activity of teaching and learning languages. Some language policies seem to be merely a topic of conversation among policy-makers concerned more with debating abstract questions or rival social visions, and distant from the reality of school life. Some policies are communicatively naïve and the nation they depict is a remembered and idealised homogenous entity, rather than the actually existing multilingual one. Often the anticipated outcome of a policy is, at face value at least, unlikely to result from its interventions. Prominent among the broad aims of Australian language policy have been: a historical reconciliation with Indigenous[1] people; new forms of citizenship, in which a robust multiculturalism replaces some sort of Anglophone solidarity (linked either to Britain or to the United States); and, most radically, a new construction of Australia as an Asian country, or at least an 'Asia-literate' society.

Espousing such aims for the mere work of teaching languages in mainstream schools certainly complies with Cooper's requirement that to understand language policy we need a 'satisfactory theory' of social change; however, if the latter seemed beyond the field's capability in the late 1980s, it is not our expectation that we can offer such a theory here. Instead, we see the volume as fulfilling some of the spadework needed to move towards linking policy and practice. The work of schools is not simply the implementation of received policies, but is an integral part of a wider activity of language planning. Understanding the links (of whatever nature) between language education and social change requires work conducted at two levels simultaneously, which may variously be expressed as: policy versus actual teaching; intention versus delivery; declared ambitions versus the realities of experience; the micro and the macro; the politician and the student; social forces and concrete interactions in classrooms.

Here we must note two limitations to the scope of the present volume. Our focus is on foreign/second/heritage languages in schooling, and not directly on issues of language and the distribution of social power, nor on the complexities of bilingualism and multiculturalism. Paradigms of analysis involving language in society are mentioned when relevant to this study but, for the most part, our orientation is to see how language education policies percolate between the authorising voices and ambitions of policy-makers, the practices of school and the responses of students. Nonetheless, it is recognised that frameworks for understanding school practices of communication – and in particular the consequences of differential access to the cultural capital represented by language – ultimately shape what a language policy may achieve. Language is intimately connected with how a society imagines itself but also with society's processes of reproduction, primarily through language's role as a vehicle for the secondary socialisation desired by the state, generally in relation to the economy and the nation. This secondary socialisation is imparted by the school, with teachers acting *in loco parentis*, whereas primary socialisation takes place within the home. For both types of socialisation the key instrument is communication, and in schooling the focus is on literate language and educated expression (Freebody, 2007; Watson-Gegeo, 2004).

Language both mediates and partly produces the social order, including its inequalities. Progressive language policies may therefore attempt to overcome inherited privilege, for instance. The proponents of such policies may be accused by conservative critics of making language education inherently ideological, but any set of social arrangements, and perhaps especially those involving communication and language, are always already 'ideological' because they reproduce and reflect an existing order, itself the outcome and accommodation of struggle and compromise among divergent interests. Certain types of knowledge, skill and behaviour will have been inherited from the past, and these or others will be privileged and rewarded in the future (Janks, 2000). What is deemed to be literate expression represents a key part of these types of knowledge, skill and behaviour. In some societies such privileging and reward are more muted than in others, and are more mutable, but, in all societies, literate expression, including multi-modal forms of expression, represents differentially distributed accumulations of cultural capital (Bourdieu, 1991).

School language practices, whether explicit and overt or implicit and unconscious, are therefore implicated in how social opportunity is negotiated and transmitted intergenerationally. Consequently, school language policies to tackle regressive practices of school language education have been proposed (Corson, 1999). For our purposes, policy analysis must always be sensitive to the connections between language and power, if it is to have any prospect of success, though the focus of the present work is not an exploration of such things so much as an account of foreign language teaching and learning in the recent Australian past. The bilingualism that results from competence in a foreign language has always been linked to power and prestige (de Mejía, 2002) and traditionally languages have claimed their place in curricula on the basis of cultural prestige. Community and heritage languages were a much later addition to the public education curriculum, not on the basis of prestige but because of pressure from newly or more actively enfranchised local communities. Moreover, the types of bilingualism and multilingualism that are produced through mass immigration, or through granting language education rights to Indigenous populations, offer the possibility of reversing or displacing one of the inherited advantages of privilege: namely, the way in which the ability to speak a foreign language signals elite cultural capital. The shifts and tensions between foreign and community/heritage constructions of languages and the potential effects of acknowledging the multiple language skills of newly arrived or socially disadvantaged populations form one of the themes of the present work.

Academic approaches to understanding language as a social practice – as a body of semiotic resources deployed interactionally – have produced important insights into how both social relations and human communication actually operate (Duranti, 2007; Gumperz & Hymes, 1972). In this body of work the focus shifts from language as an abstract system to language as a local practice for accomplishing specific aims, where 'language' is seen as a repertoire of genres, registers and varieties, and the focus is on what is 'done' rather than on what is imagined ought to be done. This is very much the focus of foreign language teaching, since, traditionally, foreign language teachers have 'represented' the community of speakers of the target language, and that community was assumed to be absent from the world surrounding the learners. Multiculturalism has, though, made many of these assumptions unstable, since 'foreign' languages are often present in the community of the learners, and this has multiple pedagogical and sociological implications (Byram & Risager, 1999).

In relation to the teaching of foreign languages, the academic literature on ethnographic research into bilingualism (Heller, 2007) and the work on interactional sociolinguistics have drawn attention to the ways in which ideas that have been inherited from the traditional academic discipline of linguistics, and in particular applied linguistics, are increasingly untenable. Indeed, the very notion of 'foreign languages' – languages as 'bounded entities', 'national languages' separated from each other and identified by discrete and homogenous cultures – is undermined by actual communication in multicultural societies at a time of rapid and deep globalisation, as well as by the prevalence of social media and instantaneous communication technologies.

Foreign language teaching is being transformed in deep ways. All these changes open up new spaces for an exploration of how language education could operate and how language policies could be designed. While we do make reference to insightful and important ways to understand language, communication and teaching, the focus in the present volume is elsewhere. We are more concerned with policy-making, and specifically with how policies are received, perceived and enacted in schools and among learners. Their responses to the aims and assumptions of policies are in effect responses to the intentions of policy-makers. We also look at the interpretations of policy by those who debate or contest policy. We discuss the chain of links in the context of four schools and their students studying Italian and Japanese under the remit of Australian language policies which yoke language education to some rather ambitious society-changing agendas.

Note

1. It is conventional in Australia to capitalise Indigenous at all times.

1 Remaking a Nation Through Language Policy

there is nothing more difficult to take in hand, more perilous to conduct,
or more uncertain in its success, than to take the lead in the introduction
of a new order of things. Because the innovator has for enemies all those
who have done well under the old conditions and lukewarm defenders
in those who may do well under the new....
Niccolò Machiavelli, 1515: *The Prince*, Chapter VI

Texts, Debate, Behaviour

The Machiavelli quote underscores the view, too often neglected in
language planning theory, that making and implementing language policies
is a political act, intended to introduce a 'new order of things'. Any desired
'new order' will give rise to a complicated and shifting group of positions,
in both support and opposition. Success will depend on cleverness of design
and on pragmatic constraints, but also on the interplay between supporters
and opponents. In this work we focus on language planning in Australia and
the introduction of two particular new orders of things: Asia literacy and
multiculturalism. The first is an umbrella term used to describe the linguistic reconstruction of Australia as linked to Asia, of Australia as a 'part of'
Asia or of Australia as having a population of citizens who know about and
identify with 'the region'. The second is also an umbrella term, one which
has aimed to reconstruct Australian society as culturally and linguistically
plural, or, rather, to invoke policies that reflect and sustain the demographic
pluralism of the population. To some readers it will appear that these are
essentially the same, or varieties of the same, vision. However, in the specific
context of Australia the two policy ambitions of Asia literacy and multiculturalism have different origins, different audiences, different histories and a

complex and not always comfortable history of interaction. At times they have constituted antagonistic policy discourses, while at other times they have been complementary visions of social improvement.

The term 'language policy' is not as straightforward as it first appears. Mostly we look for something called 'policy' on or about 'language' in laws, constitutions or regulations. But governments, states and regulations are not the sole means by which and where language teaching is influenced and regulated. If we look deeper, it soon becomes clear that decisions influencing language teaching are made outside the realm of government or officialdom. In the present discussion we are concerned only with the recent history and current reality of second language education, but it should be acknowledged at the outset that all language policy actions are ultimately interrelated, so that decisions about English and communication in general cannot be divorced from decisions about minority or foreign languages. While it is certainly true that language policy is usually located in official texts, that is, in the laws, proclamations and regulations, it is too limiting to take these as the totality of what constitutes language policy. Much analysis of language education policy is weakened by relying on such a narrow view of where language policy is made and by whom.

To get a clearer picture of language policy it is important to extend analysis to include public debates, civil society discourse and citizen advocacy. This is especially clear when debate or public action contradicts or only half-heartedly supports what official texts declare. This more in-clusive view of where language policy resides also renders analysis of its effects more realistic, because taking official statements as the sum total of language policy provides only a mechanistic account of what is really going on in practice, and reduces teachers and administrators to the status of mere implementers of external plans. Including debates and discourse in our interpretation of what constitutes language policy is, however, still insufficient, because language policy, as this volume shows, is also made in the personal communicative behaviours of individuals and groups. Actual language behaviours – what people do when speaking or not speaking in particular ways, what teachers and students actually do in classroom inter-action – is a neglected part of much language policy analysis. This wider view we call 'language planning policy', an approach that embraces all levels and layers where the intention to change language is encountered.

The language choices and attitudes of critical parties – teachers as imple-menters of language policy and learners as subjects and objects of language plans, but also parents and community members – form a complex ecological ensemble of communication choices essential to a comprehensive account of language planning. Whether these parties are adult citizens, students or new arrivals (i.e. current full members of the polity or future ones), their linguistic choices, in English and in the target languages of public policy, are like sovereign acts of decision-making, offering models available to be emulated or rejected by others. The daily interaction between those tasked to implement policy and those expected to acquire the skills envisaged by policy is a semi-autonomous domain where language use patterns are never entirely the result of official texts or public discourse alone, but are shaped and developed in local interaction, as well as in the professional roles occupied by the participants, and are influenced by the lived world of ordinary interaction in the communities in which the schools are located (Lo Bianco, 2010a, 2010b).

Intention, interpretation, implementation

Here we are proposing a dynamic model of analysis of this network of 'language planning policy'. The entire process can be seen as a chain of texts around intended language futures: texts with authority, issued by categories of people charged juridically with the control of public resources; texts of debate, interpretation, contestation or affirmation of the official texts; and texts of implementation and reception, but which have the power to confirm, modify and even subvert or redirect the language policy plans. Official texts distil decisions and are issued by bodies with formally constituted authority to allocate resources and manage implementation. Debates and discussion about those texts or rival ones arise because the official texts require public legitimacy and confirmation to succeed. The texts of implementation and reception are mainly those of professional categories of implementers – teachers and others – but, importantly, also of students, and these texts include communications in schools and in the community. That is, these three levels – the official, the civic and the interpersonal – are respectively manifested as formal texts, iterative debate and communicative behaviour. The formal texts are declarations of intention; iterative debate involves interpretation and refinement, confirmation or modification, repudiation or subversion; while actual experience in the form of communicative behaviour in schooling encompasses a wide range of activity, from realisation and full enactment, through half-heartedness and formulaic implementation, all the way to subversion and transgression. Each of the three levels is discussed in the present volume with the intention of providing a rounded account of current second language education planning in Australia.

The present chapter sets the scene for a detailed examination of language education planning as enacted in schools, a domain often far removed from the direct influence of policy-makers. Much of the evidence reported in later chapters was collected through a methodology called Q-research but also in focus groups, interviews and observations. The data serve to move the discussion of language policy into classrooms and the daily lives of learners. In our understanding, the school (or, more minutely, the classroom; and, most minutely, the interaction between teacher and learner) is a practice of language policy-making encompassed in the third modality proposed above. In her ethnography of language planning in Luxembourg, Davis (1994) identified levels similar to ours. This tiny country had seen a shift from an industrial to a service-based economy and from the stable and traditional trilingualism of French, German and Lëtzebuergesch to a dynamic, globally oriented and migrant-influenced multilingualism. The economic changes, especially the labour mobility of services, rewarded a wider and deeper set of language skills, and created a need for institutions to supply these to the labour market. Davis notes major disjunctures between three layers of language policy: its expression, essentially a set of intentions, at the national/official level; its implementation at the school level; and how policy was experienced, specifically how it differed in the lives of upper-, middle- and lower-class families. In general, elites embraced the official policy and met with success. In contrast, lower-class schoolchildren (from families lacking the necessary cultural capital and material resources) had a radically different experience: the more demanding language policy was interpreted negatively and rejected; it came to mark their exclusion from institutions and alienation.

The three levels of language policy and planning – intention, implementation and experience – traversed in this volume are mutually constituting, or interacting, though over different time frames. For example, it tends to be only over the medium to longer term that what occurs at the level of implementation comes to influence what the policy intentions declare. This can happen through politics and argument, or through programme evaluation and review, so both citizens and professionals generate texts of assessment and judgement to inform debate and discussion and ultimately influence policy intentions. Public debate and discourse are an 'agitational space' filled with vested interests, professional and political, who engage in argument to modify what the official texts say and influence what the implementers do.

In the Luxembourg case, the new language policy was expanding an existing official and society-wide multilingualism. Australia's policy tills more arid and problematic soil. Australia's multilingualism is stratified hierarchically and is intergenerationally vulnerable. For the most part, it resides among immigrants and Indigenous people, and in both cases this bilingualism is vulnerable to language shift and loss. The bilingualism of professionals such as language teachers is not usually passed on intergenerationally, and in any case is numerically small. The official domains of society, and the 'mainstream' population, remain monolingual (in English). This pattern of distribution of language abilities is broadly common to English-speaking countries. Policy intentions in the Australian setting are further complicated by the overlapping jurisdiction for education (state and federal) and contradictory policy signals, whereas Luxembourg's policy intentions were succinct and precise, although in both cases the socio-economic circumstances of schools and families play a critical role. In Australia, differences at the level of intention are compounded at the level of implementation.

Again, the third layer of policy refers to how it is experienced differentially by various groups and individuals, and is treated in a dynamic and reflexive way in this book. We access this through Q-methodology, which allows us to probe the deep feelings and responses of learners to the experience of language learning, that is, to the implementation of the plans of the policy-makers. The relation of the policy levels, and especially the interaction between intentions and experiences, mediated by interpretation, forms the central argument of the book. It explores aspects of agency, argument, alienation and the complexity of the lived world of school language teaching and learning, the arguments surrounding it and the desires of the 'far away' writers of policy reports.

Language policies in non-English-dominant nations are supported by much less justificatory rhetoric to persuade learners to be interested in language learning, whereas in English-speaking settings a predictable feature of language policy texts, raised constantly in public debate, are arguments rehearsing the value of language learning, always dealing directly or implicitly with the disincentive posed by the international demand for English. Advocates of multilingualism tend to adopt a range of argumentative strategies, such as minimising or critiquing the world role of English, or acknowledging it but citing instances in which English monolingualism is disadvantageous (for example in trade negotiations or security arrangements), or projecting a decline in the future importance of English, or arguing that the primary reasons for learning languages are cultural, intellectual and humanistic.

These efforts to justify the teaching and learning of languages sometimes merge into claims about the need for a more equitable global communication arrangement, demanding that English native speakers take more responsibility, a 'fairer share of the load' as one teacher described it to us. Indeed, a desire to bring about a more fairly distributed global communication effort is often present in both declared policy and the conceptions of teachers enacting language policy in schools. In the Australian case, language learning has also deployed an additional series of legitimations, invoking new kinds of citizenship and new formations of national identity. A dramatic recent instalment was the Australia 2020 Summit, a national 'visioning' exercise which took place on 19–20 April 2008 (discussed below) and which represented a stark display of how language learning, especially Asian language study, has come to represent a deep-seated ambition to create a new and desirable national character, a unique amalgam of moral purpose, economic destiny and political security.

Australia is perhaps not unique in this respect; language education policies often imply or explicitly aim to direct national futures in particular ways. The language choices of any nation reveal whom the interlocutors for future citizens are imagined to be, and the level of investment in a programme suggests which party in imagined future relationships will be expected to make the greater effort to facilitate communication. What is perhaps unique to Australia, other than the particular mix of languages involved, is the frequency with which new imagined futures and new imagined future citizens have been invoked in language policy. For instance, Lo Bianco and Gvozdenko (2006) identified 67 language education statements, plans, policies or declarations at the federal level in the preceding four decades. Also possibly unique to Australia is how ambitious, and often how unrealistic, have been the aims of language policy. The disparity between intention and implementation exposes the critical mediating role of the interpretation, the debate, argument and discourse that surround public texts and that influence school implementation. Exposing the gap between the intentions of policy-makers and the achievement in schools of the aims of policy also opens up language policy-making to a new kind of analysis, one which sees schools and schooling, and the actors located there (teachers and learners principally), as agents capable of far more effect on language planning than those charged with issuing policy statements acknowledge. This is one of the reasons we have selected to focus the current analysis at the three levels of intention, interpretation and implementation.

As stated, public discussion of language education options reveals something of a community's vision of its future conversations, whom its future citizens will be speaking to, since, ultimately, language learning aims to facilitate interaction with others, and language plans are based on the priority selections from all possible interactants. This selection of potential future conversational partners for 'modern' languages reverses the classical construction of 'conversation' partners, in which the choice of the languages of the past, Latin principally in western societies, involved accessing past texts to listen in on past conversations, with socially improving and moral purposes in the present. Language education plans therefore reveal the working out of our ideas about preferred interlocutors, those deemed most profitable, admirable or probable, and so language education planning is an activity with wide-ranging cultural, ideological and even moral implications.

The Problem of English and Global Communication

English is a problem for foreign language educators in English-speaking countries. In a study of the role of English in school curricula across the world over the past 155 years Cha and Ham (2008) show how it overtook its expansionist European rivals, French and German, to dominate language education choices (see also Byram *et al.*, 2010). Cha and Ham's survey of world foreign language choices serves as a reminder of two critically important facts: that the high prevalence of English is relatively recent, and that language education choices are tied to 'world events'. The fortunes of French and German, the rivals of English since the middle of the 19th century, have fluctuated according to the economic, political and military turbulence of international relations. The shifts were most dramatic at the end of the First and Second World Wars and the end of the Cold War with the symbolically resonant collapse of the Berlin Wall (Table 1.1). At each of these junctures German ceded to French and French to English, with only an interval of presence for Russian in the latter two periods. The number of countries represented in the data increased from 15 and 12 for primary and secondary schools in 1850–74, to 151 and 154 for 1990–2005. In Asia, the proportion of schools with English on their curriculum grew from 33% of primary schools during 1945–69 to 83% by 2005; by 2005 all the Asian secondary schools taught English. For an extended discussion of Cha and Ham's survey, see Lo Bianco and Slaughter (2009).

Table 1.1 World foreign language choices in education: Overall percentage of schools (primary and secondary) offering German, French or English

Period	German	French	English
1850–74	50.0	33.3	8.3
1875–99	44.4	38.9	5.6
1900–19	24.3	45.9	27.0
1920–44	14.8	35.2	33.3
1945–69	00.0	28.1	59.4
1970–89	00.0	17.0	67.4
1990–2005	00.7	13.6	82.1

Adapted from Cha and Ham (2008).

At about the beginning point of Cha and Ham's survey, the mid-19th century, intellectuals in Europe perceived the onset of a global age and some idealists began to create artificial languages, as they anticipated, incorrectly, that the world would prefer a neutral, invented code to the national languages of the Great Powers. Within a century and a half, most invented languages had been relegated to the private preoccupations of individual enthusiasts, the exception being Esperanto, which has achieved admirable though limited spread. English, the language of one of those Great Powers, or rather of two, has prevailed decisively over French and German, leading Cha and Ham to speculate that a 'single global' English-mediated society might be emerging.

However, there are various interpretations of these and similar data, or extrapolations from them, and of the link between auxiliary languages and 'world events'. For instance, Nicholas Ostler interprets the comings and goings of dominant languages in his *Empires of the Word* (2005), a 5000-year linguistic history of the world. In a later work he compares the fate and fortunes of global English with its closest parallel, Latin (Ostler, 2007); and more recently he reflects on English as the 'last lingua franca' (Ostler, 2010). The much longer historical perspective and the specific comparison lead him to propose that instead of ubiquitous English, in place of the 'single global society' envisaged by Cha and Ham, a technology-mediated 'return of Babel' (Ostler, 2010) is emerging. This depiction of English as the 'last lingua franca' departs from what we could call the 'inevitabilist' school, who take for granted the view that English has prevailed (or will prevail), represented by Abraam De Swaan (1993) and others, who imagine a global English denuded of national interest and ideology, a fully utilitarian vehicle for global and convenient exchange, and who specifically reject questioning of this vision as an act of linguistic 'sentimentalism'. De Swaan's (2004) analysis proposes that English derives its lingua franca status from what he labels its Q-value, that is, its generative power, essentially the predictable number of interlocutors, settings, texts and so on available in English compared with the Q-value of other languages. The great Q-value of English supplies a greater 'return on investment' to learners. This view pleases 'the Anglosphere' (Bellocchio, 2006; Bennett, 2004), which wants to view English and the culture it animates as exceptional and which makes a virtue of the transactional functions of English (cultural neutrality) while still asserting some nested values (cultural positivity) for it, specifically free enterprise and representative democracy. So, in this conception, English is both neutral and not neutral: it is neutral when Anglosphere argumentation wants to minimise potential resistance to global English; and not neutral when the values claimed for English coincide with the key interests of the main English-speaking powers.

The politics of Asian engagement in Australia differ from the global moves in recent years to promote Chinese teaching and to adapt to the progressive transfer of economic wealth to the Asian region. In a thorough analysis of how academic intellectuals and policy-makers interacted to forge Australia's brand of Asia engagement, Beeson and Jayasuriya (2009) document a distinctive 'policy turn in academic studies that reflected the triumph of neoliberalism and the waning of ideological politics of the 1960s' (p. 373) which marked shifts from Cold War positions and alliances Australia would make to direct international engagement with Asian powers. For these writers, Asian engagement is a 'mirror' of 'anxieties and vulnerabilities' but also a reflection of debates about the national and political identity of a 'settler society that is both "in and out" of its immediate region' (p. 374; see also Harries, 1993), an Anglosphere nation in Asia with a multicultural population. They document a struggle between conservative and radical depictions of and approaches to Asia, and identify a 'public culture' which has allowed key academic figures to move between political and policy-making circles and academic research domains, shaping ideas, understandings and interpretations of events, purposes and relations. This analysis can be extended back in time; the authors note the role of intellectuals, as producers of ideas and as advisers to governments, in shaping positions with regard to the two great interest groups for language and cultural diversification in education: Indigenous populations and immigrant groups. Thus, policy is shaped by what intellectual/academic elites believe about the purposes of language learning, about English in the world, about bilingualism and minority languages and about what citizenship action can achieve in the face of entrenched beliefs.

After the fall of the Berlin Wall there was a wave of theorising about the future of the world. This was a moment of immense optimism about the Anglosphere and its prescription of liberal capitalist democratic nation states, iconically expressed by American political scientist Francis Fukuyama (1992) as 'the end of history'; however, it was given more overt cultural and linguistic shape in *The Anglosphere Challenge* (Bennett, 2004), a book about the unique virtues claimed for the legal traditions and cultural values of English-speaking nations. According to James Bennett, the Anglosphere is a precise entity, not a nation, or even a group of nations, or a trans-national institution, but a 'network civilisation', which, though lacking a political structure, has grown from the traditions of England to the expanded post-colonial English-speaking nations to spread to proximal areas. But because the nations that comprise the Anglosphere are extremely diverse in culture and tradition, the values and political ideologies attached to speaking English are controversial, in part owing to an excessive linguistic determinism. For example, the two key parties of the Anglosphere, the United States and Britain, were forged in their separation from each other, in war and revolution, so that the founding of one was premised on the rejection of some characteristics (principally monarchy) of the other.

The Anglosphere formulations were in fact clearly premature, as well as self-congratulatory, inured from alternative visions and criticisms, and sustained by apologist history (Roberts, 2006). Moreover, predictions of Anglosphere domination failed utterly to anticipate the 'emergence of China' (Lo Bianco, 2007) and the loss of confidence and political traction for the United States that have followed the global financial crisis of 2008. More critical is Bellocchio's (2006) analysis, in which the Anglosphere is based on the 'soft power' victory of the United States after Second World War and also the powerful triumph of Britain in preventing the unification of continental Europe, thereby shifting the locus of geo-strategic power to the Atlantic. His analysis, however, is also sensitive to the shift, currently underway, from Atlantic to Pacific, from uni- or bi-polar geo-politics to a multi-polar world in which the Anglosphere is not hegemonic.

What is clear is that, today, English lacks a single rival, though rhetorically Chinese is sometimes called 'the new English'. The Anglosphere assumption that English has transcended the classic 'conquest and conversion' phase of language expansion, to have entered a politically neutral phase of commerce, is rebutted by Ostler's argument about the great expense of maintaining a lingua franca, when a technology-enabled 'Babel' is imminent. But perhaps, as Lo Bianco et al. (2009) show, in China, where it matters most, English struggles to transcend its 'foreignness' and association with the cultural and ideological interests of the west in the views of many Chinese. Clearest evidence of this is how often Chinese patriotism is invoked as legitimation for compulsory English learning, in a pragmatic acceptance of today's linguistic order only in the interests of advancing China's future.

Projecting future communication patterns on the basis of past ones assumes that conditions remain comparable and that new or radically different possibilities do not emerge, and yet processes of globalisation and instantaneous technology-facilitated communication are likely to disrupt present communication patterns. The emergence of a globally linked world, through technology-mediated communication, has already influenced both speech and writing in unpredictable ways. The idea of a 'return of Babel' is a radical depiction of the linguistic consequences of globalisation, a future of technology-facilitated multilingual exchange, a communication order in which 'everyone will speak and write in whatever language they choose' (Ostler, 2010). This image of communication technologies tied to social media and the prospect of intercultural communication without the added cost of acquiring proficiency in a second language proposes not a 'new English' such as Chinese, but an end to mediating languages altogether, and so imagines English as the 'last lingua franca'. Essentially, this vision requires communication beyond a convenient common auxiliary language, selected through real-world 'hard power' (military and economic), based on mediation tools and processes that offer greater convenience, rapidity, accuracy, fluency and naturalness than those currently offer. This is not the place to evaluate the prospects of such apparently utopian plurilingualism; the question is, though, impressively surveyed in Ostler's volume, and supported elsewhere, such as by research into cognate language comprehension and teaching programmes. In the latter case, at least, research on inter-comprehension across the individual languages in three European language groupings, Germanic, Romance and Slavonic, is well advanced and theoretically and experimentally sophisticated (see http://www.eurocom-frankfurt.de).

It is likely that language policy decision-making in China, at the levels of intention, interpretation and implementation, planners, citizens and teachers, will influence the fate not just of the Chinese language and its global role but also of English. What is undeniable from the data comparing choice of first foreign language (FFL) in the curricula of primary and secondary schools is volatility (Table 1.1), reflecting momentous changes in the world over the past century and a half, and much more deeply in the longer historical survey. Present arrangements cannot be assumed to be secure. Policy-makers worldwide have determined that Chinese is the big 'up and comer' (Lo Bianco, 2010a) and that its effects will be deep and pervasive, hence today's recurring language policy argument even in English-speaking countries such as Britain and Australia, where advocates struggle against complacency, and parents and teachers are advised to 'never mind French and Spanish' (Ward, 2007).

The party politics of Australian language planning

In the Australian context, a perverse benefit of the global role of English is to remove most practical or utilitarian imperatives from language study, such as characterise second language education rationales in most non-English-speaking nations. Although this means that *any* second language is theoretically selectable for teaching, economic utilitarianism remains a strong feature of the reasoning in support of language education. Potentially undermining this utilitarian case for foreign language education, though, is a business case: public education, especially in universities but increasingly in schools, has for two decades generated substantial revenue from English.

This commodification of English is fostered in separate government policies from foreign language teaching, usually policies of trade promotion and higher education administration; and is not generally considered 'language policy', but the 'commercialisation' or 'export' of education.

In language policy texts the phrases 'the region' and 'our region' act as important cultural signifiers, organising the way Australians have come to accommodate to their Asia Pacific geography in recent decades (Lo Bianco, 2004). Japanese is the language that crystallises the national choice for regionalism perfectly, while Italian is the language that most sharply crystallises the previous phase of domestic multiculturalism. Both arise in language policy as part of self-conscious policy styling, that is, as attempts to remake national identity: in the case of Japanese as part of a programme called 'Asia literacy'; and in the case of Italian as part of a programme of multiculturalism, which in the 1970s involved distancing the nation from British cultural roots and American cultural influence. Multiculturalism further sought to exploit immigration-derived domestic pluralism and to combine it with a growing consciousness of Indigenous history as resources in debates about national identity.

The data-gathering period for the study presented in this book, 2005–11, is set within a longer historical framework, and specifically the multiculturalism phase of policy originating with the Labour government of Prime Minister Gough Whitlam in the early to mid-1970s. The study's setting is the western suburbs of Melbourne in the state of Victoria, a large, multi-ethnic, immigrant and industrial area, containing pockets of middle-class housing. In a possibly unique development among comparable countries, the Whitlam government's steps towards formalising multiculturalism as a policy project were continued, even strengthened, by its replacement conservative Liberal–National Party government led by Malcolm Fraser from 1975. This meant that some form of multicultural education became a shared project of public life in Australia. However, even the shorter time frame during which the school research was conducted (2005–11) featured considerable change in political direction at both federal and state (Victorian) level and in language political priorities and ideologies. During this seven-year period there were three Premiers of the state of Victoria (Stephen Bracks to 2007, John Brumby to 2010, both from the Australian Labour Party, and Ted Baillieu, leader of the Liberal–National Coalition, from December 2010). At the federal level, politics took the reverse direction, with the Liberal–National government with John Howard as Prime Minister (March 1996 to December 2007) replaced by the Prime Ministership of Kevin Rudd (on 24 October 2007), who in turn was replaced in an internal Australian Labour Party move by Julia Gillard (on 24 June

2010). Gillard is the 27th Prime Minister and, after replacing Rudd, called an early election on 21 August 2010, at which the Australian Labour Party lost its majority but later formed a coalition government with the Greens and three Independent Members of the House of Representatives (sworn in on 14 September 2010). Rudd served as Prime Minister for 2 years and 204 days and then as Foreign Minister in the Gillard government; he lost a challenge for the leadership in February 2012. Rudd is the most prominent speaker of Mandarin Chinese in the nation and a long-time advocate of priority for Asian languages. In 1994 he was critical in pushing federal and state governments to adopt a national strategy for Asian languages; the four chosen were Chinese, Indonesian, Japanese and Korean, determined on the basis of volumes of trade and, in the case of Indonesian, geographical proximity. Ongoing jostling for power between Rudd and Gillard actually conditioned the latter's own interest in Asian integration and language education, as she possibly sought to staunch a public image advantage held by her rival. Political reporter Michele Grattan (2011) has even speculated that a 'resurrected Rudd' could inherit the policy Gillard promoted partly to keep him at bay politically. This rather bizarre source of innovation must be unprecedented in the annals of language policy.

On the whole, though, Australian politicians are notoriously monolingual, as evidenced by the only study of their language competencies and language learning biographies (Lo Bianco, 2007). The evidence comes from their responses to a survey questionnaire administered to a sample of members of all nine legislative structures in Australia: those of the six states and the two territories, and the federal parliament. The vast majority had no or only the most rudimentary knowledge of languages other than English. For those who did have such skills, the research found that they tended to personalise their positions on language issues, so that Members of Parliament with direct experience of language study, or who were of non-English-speaking background, were predictably more likely to make speeches addressing language issues and in doing so to display their experience and knowledge of languages in these speeches. While their voting tendencies typically followed party lines, language-aware politicians were more likely to support language causes in general, or they claimed their language connections as the basis for finding fault in proposals they were required to reject. In the majority of cases, direct multilingual experiences made them more sympathetic to minority issues, though not always; sometimes their support wavered according to judgements about the practical utility of one or other language or group of languages. These tended to lead parliamentarians to oppose positive moves for multilingualism if that multilingualism was seen to be generated from 'sentimental' or 'advocacy' reasons, or if it could not be otherwise linked explicitly to a notion of 'the national interest'.

In many debates Members (of the House of Representatives) and Senators foregrounded stories of their own personal experiences, or of those of their families and friends, and of individual constituents. These constituents were often named and used to exemplify a principle of good citizenship, invoking economic benefits or virtuous social behaviour. Underlying much of this discourse was an implicit need to repudiate any implication that recognition of multilingualism leads to social fragmentation, divided loyalties or economic dependency. Many conservatives claimed the home as the secure and proper site for fostering language knowledge, while many Labour members attached that responsibility to public education. Members of Parliament of immigrant origin, those who were of Indigenous background or who represented Indigenous constituents and those who had been teachers or who had lived in non-English-speaking countries invariably cited these experiences to validate languages, bilingualism and multiculturalism.

However, these were minority positions overall. For the most part, the research revealed a deep disparity between the widespread multilingualism of Australian society and the shallow depth and narrow range of the linguistic backgrounds among the nation's parliamentarians. The exceptions were few and notable. It is from this largely monolingual and generally linguistically unrepresentative group, the nation's parliamentarians, that the official texts of language policy are generated.

In the next sections we survey the spheres of official texts (intention) and debate (interpretation) in policy, to lay the groundwork for discussion of implementation at the school level in subsequent chapters.

Official Texts (Intention)

During the writing of this book, three official texts 'reigned' as language policies at the national level in Australia, each aiming to introduce a 'new order of things'. The contradictions, lack of integration and differential status of these three separate texts are stark. The failure to reconcile and integrate them implies that, at the level of macro policy-making, the state lacks the guidance of expert language planners, and suggests that the political framework for policy-making on languages is one of accommodating to and placating diverse constituencies and interests.

In reviewing these texts it becomes clear how language policy analysis must shift attention away from exclusive reliance on official plans and include consideration of the role of debate and public discourse in interpreting and framing action, and on the behaviours and communicative choices in the realm of implementation, to obtain an accurate depiction of what really constitutes a nation's language plans and commitments. This point will become clearer as the relationship between the three official coexisting language policy declarations is described.

These three texts were produced by the federal government through its Department of Education, Employment and Workplace Relations, though in all cases they were negotiated with that Department's equivalent bodies at state and territory level. Each of these is discussed in turn below: the *National Statement and Plan for Languages*; the *National Indigenous Languages Policy*; and the *National Asian Languages and Studies in Schools Program*.

(1) *National Statement and Plan for Languages*

This policy document (in full the *National Statement for Languages Education in Australian Schools; National Plan for Languages Education in Australian Schools*) was a shared official text issued jointly by the education ministers across the country (Ministerial Council on Education, Employment, Training and Youth Affairs, 2005). It comprises a declaration of the purpose and nature of languages education, general legitimations for language study and indications of funding support from the federal government, negotiated separately in annual budgets, with allocations made to all education jurisdictions (government and non-government) on the basis of enrolled numbers of students. In essence, then, this is a national and system-wide declaration on languages and therefore constitutes a national language plan.

The document adopts the language of inclusion, and argues that there are multiple reasons for learning languages and that the choice of language taught should be negotiated with parents, teachers and students. This spirit of all-encompassing and inclusive ideology is epitomised by statements such as 'all languages are equally valid', 'learners gain similar social, cognitive, linguistic and cultural benefits, regardless of the language studied' and 'Australian Indigenous languages have a unique place in Australia's heritage and in its cultural and educational life'.

(2) *The National Indigenous Languages Policy*

Issued on 9 August 2009 jointly by the federal Education Minister and the Minister for Indigenous Affairs (Macklin & Garrett, 2009), this statement aimed to direct support to Indigenous Australians to 'connect with their language, culture and country' and to address the 'problem of language loss'. The declaration was intended to foster national attention on 'the oldest surviving languages in the world', to prevent their 'decline and extend use as much as possible', to 'close the gap' (i.e. to link language education to the aim of lessening the inequalities of Indigenous people), to strengthen pride in identity and culture, through 'restoration of rarely spoken languages', and to 'offer indigenous languages as second languages in schools'. The statement consisted of a series of such declarations of support but only a small amount of funding was allocated to their realisation; however, in light of what is known about serious language revival efforts (Fishman, 2001) the chance of this programme making a significant contribution to reversing the shift was negligible. Unfortunately, during the life of the programmes supported by the policy, the standing of Indigenous languages in education deteriorated markedly; for instance, public bilingual programmes in the Northern Territory, where the largest number of speakers and languages are located, were required to ensure that the first four hours of the school day were delivered exclusively in English (Simpson *et al.*, 2009).

Exactly a decade earlier, in the only major discussion in the Australian parliament on Indigenous languages (Lo Bianco, 1999), we find a clear example of language policy being constructed in debate as well as in the announced statements contained in official texts as issued by those with authority and control of resources. In this particular instance, a parliamentary question about the violation of human rights (involving the undermining of bilingual education) produced an agreement among parliamentarians (with the collusion of the Speaker of the House) that interpreted bilingual education as a form of English literacy!

(3) *National Asian Languages and Studies in Schools Program* (NALSSP)

The third text of official language policy was a brief, economics-based announcement of a funding programme, organised around date-governed achievement targets for both numbers and proficiency, a level of specificity missing from the previous two statements. The target was that by 2020 'at least 12%' of students would complete their final year of schooling (year 12) with 'a fluency in one of the target Asian languages (Mandarin, Indonesian, Japanese and Korean) sufficient for engaging in trade and commerce in Asia and/or university study' (vol. 2: 1). It was almost universally acknowledged that achieving this target was highly improbable and during 2010 a series of policy reports (see Lo Bianco & Slaughter, 2009) and studies of language performance underscored serious underperformance against the target. Even if numerical targets could be achieved, the proficiency aims were unrealistic in light of the typical standard of school Asian language programmes. Among the financing and initiatives supported were 'additional Asian languages

classes in high schools, teacher training' and the 'development of [a] specialist curriculum for students who display advanced abilities'.

The relationship between the three language policy declarations

The existence of three unintegrated policy statements suggests that each
was directed to a separate political constituency, was championed by different supporters and responded to different interests. The first, the National
Statement and Plan, responded to the widest constituency, a professional-
and community-based interest, concerned with universal language teaching,
rather than any particular group of languages, and with cultural, humanistic
and pluralistic rationales in the main. According to the argument, English
furnishes Australian education with the possibility of choosing multiple
second languages, without having to draw a sharp priority on the basis of
instrumental justifications for this or that particular one.

Of the three, only the announcement of the NALSSP was accompanied by substantial financial allocations and the policy was the only
one organised around measurable targets. The significance of this is due to
how public administration works: targets make precise evaluation possible
and even necessary, and evaluations are critical in establishing new policy.
Evaluations of practice support debate about improvement and while this
is possible with any policy formulation, vaguer formulations tend to have
weaker policy traction. The NALSSP was first funded in the 2008–09 federal
budget, for three years (i.e. scheduled to terminate mid-2012), to the tune of
$62.4 million per annum, with the funds directed to school programmes in
Chinese, Indonesian, Japanese and Korean. In the 2011–12 budget, without
fanfare or announcement, no ongoing funding for the programme was
included, suggesting that it, too, would not be renewed, though (diminish-
ing) amounts of funding remained to allow completion of existing projects.
No clear reason was given; there were just mooted points that Asian languages would continue to attract support.

Anecdotal evidence circulated that the NALSSP was weakened by the
large disparity between its high aims (numbers and proficiency) and the low
likelihood of their achievement. During 2011, as the scheduled term of the
NALSSP drew to a close, it became clear by observing the lobbying for its
continuation that targets, however problematical from other points of view,
are a requirement of policy-making conversations. Failure to achieve targets
is a logical entry point for reporters and interviewers discussing language
policy with activists, and the general idea of demanding the completion of
projects, and making up shortfalls between what was declared and what
was achieved, is a powerful dynamic in public discourse. The specificity

of the text, despite its unrealistic aims, supplied its supporters with the argumentative and conceptual tools appropriate to policy formulation, and allowed the mainstream media access to the argumentative routine of advocating completion. None of these qualities is available to the lobbyists who want to advance more general language policy, or for Indigenous language activists, who must make do with arguments of moral suasion, political pressure or overcoming disadvantage, all of which, regardless of their merits, play less well in mainstream media advocacy than economics-based reasoning. Advocacy for Asian languages gravitates around questions of commercial engagement, security arrangements, geographical proximity and an 'inevitabilist' logic about how the large-scale shift of trading and strategic power to Asia is long term, indeed is part of the 'Asian century'. The apogee of this reasoning is the text of the Gillard-commissioned review of Australia's relations with Asia, *Australia in the Asian Century*, released as a White Paper in October 2012 (Australian Government, 2012).

Finally, the Indigenous languages statement exposes the limits of traction available to policy-makers, since the achievement of most of its aims, and certainly language revival and restoration, rests with community arrangements, not with government. A detailed consideration of this question is, however, beyond the scope of the present volume.

It is also worth mentioning that the kind of language planning involved in these three official texts is radically different. For Asian languages, the clear aim was economics-centred foreign language teaching. For Indigenous languages, the policy seemed to make well meaning but largely unrealistic gestures towards reversing language extinction, when the great need is for direct support to affected communities, to construct economic, social and educational activities to support intergenerational language maintenance. The National Statement and Plan, by contrast, was more directed towards language culture; the text gave educational and humanistic reasons for language study and laid out the role of languages in a comprehensive intellectually grounded curriculum.

These, then, were the three federal policies current during our research, the official texts framing language education. The next main section discusses interpretation, the second of the three modes in which language policy is constructed; implementation is the subject of later chapters. First, though, we should mention an important recent development at national level.

National curriculum (2013)

All three texts were in fact incorporated into the new Australian curriculum, progressively being implemented from 2013, itself a radical departure from how the curriculum has previously been devised in Australia, constitutionally delegated to state and education jurisdictions. In the planning for the national curriculum, languages, and not exclusively Asian languages, have been declared a priority discipline, though studies of Asia and of Indigenous culture have been prioritised as two of three cross-curricular fields ('sustainability' is the third). A large group of languages has been selected for the preparation of curriculum frameworks, commencing with Chinese and Italian.

Public Debate (Interpretation)

Language policy is also made by debate, which interprets policy or influences and modifies texts of language policy. In the absence of official texts of policy, language planning choices are made through discussion, debate and convention. The period of time under consideration, 2005–11, coincides with considerable political change. It saw the final years of the Liberal–National government of Prime Minister John Howard – which in 2002 had terminated the NALSAS (National Asian Languages and Studies in Australian Schools) strategy, a large national programme of special funding for Asian languages which preceded the NALSSP – and its defeat in November 2007 by the Rudd Labour government, as well as, in turn, his replacement by Julia Gillard as Prime Minister in June 2010, and her election as Prime Minister in August 2010 in a coalition with minority party support.

During this period, public discourse on languages was sharply focused on the perceived failure or inadequacy of Asian language policy, with the occasional challenge to the now longstanding priority of Asian languages, especially its instrumental and economic focus; however, the strongest and most insistent voices were those calling for a more serious, well funded and total national reorientation to Asia in the context of the 'Asian century'.

Our discussion of the Asian languages strategy draws upon an article by the prominent literary critic, author and journalist Luke Slattery, writing in a national newspaper, *The Australian* (a flagship of the News Limited Australian media conglomerate), who at the time was editor of its Literary Review and the Higher Education sections. This is essentially because his critique proposes an alternative set of priorities within language policy, rather than politically hostile general rejection (although examples of such rejection are also discussed below). Slattery's approach contests the overwhelming mainstream media endorsement of an Asia-centred language policy based on trade relations with Asian economies, while supporting general claims for increased Asian language capabilities in the population.

In the lead-up to the election which brought Rudd to power, Slattery (2007) devoted attention to Rudd's ideas and plans in the pages of *The Australian*. He judged Rudd's interest in language study commendable but his overall assessment of the aspiring Prime Minister's intention to introduce an exclusively Asian languages policy was that it was 'flawed'. 'To the extent that it promotes a small number of Asian languages for mercantile reasons, it is unnecessarily blinkered and possibly counterproductive.' Slattery went on to examine the outcomes of the previous strategy on Asian languages, the NALSAS programme (1994–2002), also under Rudd's tutelage, and the clear evidence of poor student retention in Asian language programmes in Rudd's home state of Queensland:

> the state that most deeply bears the stamp of Rudd's language reforms from his years as director-general of the office of cabinet under the Goss [Queensland state government] ... has the nation's lowest retention rate to Year 12[1] for students.

Slattery also lamented what he called the 'zero-sum game' thinking in language policy, and cited the late Professor Michael Clyne, prominent linguist and community language advocate, who had pointed out that the focus on Asian languages in the absence of an overarching policy for universal language study was simply replacing the students studying one language with those studying another, rather than increasing overall enrolments:

> German ... the chief casualty of the rise of Japanese.... Mandarin today is coming at the expense of Indonesian and Japanese and of some European languages.

Slattery reported that there was a:

> fear that a concerted drive on Mandarin, Japanese and Indonesian, such as Rudd and others envisage, will come at the expense of European languages and that other tongue of strategic importance, Arabic. What the country most needs, and what language experts without a personal enthusiasm for Asian literacy tend to advocate, is a broad, balanced, heterogenous group of languages and some urgent measures to boost student enrolments and teacher expertise. Rudd is a responsible moderate on most areas of public policy, but in this field he is a revolutionary. In a paper published in 1995 entitled Creating an Asia-Literate Society, he argued for nothing short of a 'radical intervention through the school system' to realise his goal of mass Asia literacy.

Slattery added educational reasoning to his case, as follows:

Rudd recognises academic research confirming that Asian languages demand three times as many contact hours as European languages to develop a comparable level of proficiency. His solution to start earlier ignores another view of language acquisition: that the most effective second language, in the sense of being easier to grasp and more profitable for learners, is one that enjoys some filial relationship with the mother tongue.

On the basis of this premise, Slattery proposed an 'apprentice tongue' policy, commencing with cognate languages and moving out to embrace Asian languages. He concluded that the 'simple reality of cognition places limits on Rudd's dream of mass Asian literacy' because 'character-based or tone languages simply do not get the same linguistic bang for their buck – or their time – as those of European languages'.

Although Slattery sought to advance a humanistic rationale for language education and to contest the commercial motivation of the day, he nonetheless found room, on 'strong pragmatic grounds', 'for French (influential in diplomacy, indispensable in the halls of the European Union and strongly represented in the Pacific), German (the economic hub of continental Europe and a core cultural language), Spanish (the world's and the US's second most widely spoken language) and Arabic (vital for reasons of security and trade)'.

The final points Slattery went on to make were about the institutional location of language education. In his view commercially oriented language teaching should be devolved to specialist providers, while school and university language teaching should rest solely on cultural and intellectual purposes. Anticipating what proved to be a critical problem, Slattery also chastised the aspiring Prime Minister for neglecting the multicultural or heritage language context. He pointed out that the nation would achieve a greater return on investment in strategically important languages by giving support to immigrant groups to run language maintenance activities within their own communities, rather than spending resources on teaching languages *ab initio* to Anglophone monolinguals who would achieve, on average, lower proficiency in Asian trade languages.

Most debate on language policy that influences and interprets official pronouncements is not so nuanced. In a polemical piece in the Melbourne newspaper the *Herald Sun* on 3 February 2011 Steve Price, a radio broadcaster on the Melbourne morning talkback station 3MTR, suggested that Australia should '*ditch*' the entire activity of language teaching (Price, 2011).

He began by citing evidence of the actual experience of students, highlighting the case of '15 year old Matthew', who had called his talkback show to express an opinion about political matters. This was a preamble for a critique of 'a Rudd-inspired policy from 2008 that pledged $62 million of taxpayers' money to force our students to learn an Asian language'. Price cited Matthew's story of having been 'taught Indonesian, followed by Italian and German, and now he was doing no languages' – an experience which 'mirrors that of my own children, now in years 7 and 8. The eldest girl, who is a straight-A student, has sat through Italian, French, Japanese, more Italian and now Latin'. Citing as fact claims about declining English standards and claiming deleterious effects of texting and the widespread use of social media, as well as poor programme implementation and inadequate coordination, Price then declared the entire endeavour of second language education futile and unnecessary.

The online comments which followed the web version of the article (Price, 2011) traverses much of the agitational terrain of the language teaching dispute, interspersed with boos and cheers. The traffic is a kind of *demos*: the political, speculative, personal, dubious, committed, quirky or non-comprehending targets of national language planning. A sample appears below, cited without change to original spelling or expression:

marty of frankston

forcing australain children to learn a foreign language confims that australia is now, and has been for a long time, a democratic dictatorship....

Priorities!

... as a teacher, I agree with you. There are so few people in the last two generations whose written English is passable, let alone good, it is pure folly to contemplate adding more languages. Put bluntly, the education system seems unable to even teach English properly so why would they be going off in other directions as well? ... It is so foolish to keep adding to a curriculum that squeezes out the basics, leaving young people deskilled and underachieving.

Tracey of Melbourne

OK Steve, then following your logic, let's ditch Science, for those looking to move into Arts or Business, or get rid of History and Geography. The study of a language introduces students to languages in general – just like many other subjects introduce their topics that may not necessarily be kept through to VCE.[2] Lets have all students chose their career path in Primary School and only teach them what is relevant to that path! Most subjects provide not only the facts and figures of their curriculum, but also teaching/learning methods that benefit not just that subject, but learning and thinking in general.

CL Angus of Richmond
You make the assumption that because Gen Y makes use of shorthand in social media they can't write or read English properly. That's complete rubbish – Gen Y is no worse than Baby Boomers or Gen X, many of whom were able to drop out of school at far younger ages than now and pick up menial jobs which required no education or brainpower. As for languages, being bilingual has been shown to substantially improve a person's study abilities. Rather than scrap languages, perhaps we should be looking at limiting them so that we have some consistency across the country.

Ricky of Barham
Thanks for your advice Mr Price. I've always believed the national curriculum should be determined by the anecdotal whimsies of pint sized shock-jocks.

Mat of South Melbourne
There are a number of flaws in this argument. The teaching of language has been around since well before Rudd became PM. I tried (and failed) to learn Italian at school over 25 years ago. The problem is that the children these days just do bites of each language. One year they may do a little bit of Chinese, the next Italian and then the next Indonesian. There is no way someone will become fluent unless they commit to a language fully.

WACD of Melbourne
I agree lets turn the time into Driver Education First Aid Defensive courses Make it a requirment to visit TAC centres visit and see the injured Really what use or these courses not to our Children in todays Time poor world Respect and Accountablilty needs to be taught again and make them learn the real hard lessons of lifes Journey Driving on our Roads and Respect the law and not the size off the motor or Speed on the Spedo Let the State and Federal Goverment for once get the start of the Kids Journey in one of the biggest challenges they have Leaners Licence and Rights of drivers and Rights of Laws in this State. Hopefully

this is brought in will save lifes Does teaching a Language in our School really now have any benefit to there future harsh words but times have changed

James P of Melbourne
Sorry Steve, you have no idea why a student is taught a second language. It is to help you understand your first language. Its a bit hard for mono lingual Aussies to understand sometimes, but studying and learning about the structure of another language makes you realised and understand things about your first language you never knew.

Jack the quipper
Fully seconded. Some of the young chimps around today have no clue about communication, language, manners, dress modes. God help Australia in the future cos Australians are going to have to learn Chines just to buy goods the way things are going.

Brendan of Melbourne
I think the money should be spent providing Steve Price with an education on SMS and Twitter slang, so he can stay in touch and not be so bitter.

FooFoo of Narnia
Yep. Another Labor experiment at our expense.

MD of Latin America
… Agree and disagree with sentiments given here. Our issue as English speakers and with our location is there is no obvious language to learn/ need (unlike most of the non-English speaking world which have an obvious need for English). You can make a decent argument for learning Mandarin, Indonesian, Japanese, Spanish and French. However, none of these (perhaps Mandarin is emerging as the exception) are a clear-cut choice as a needed language. Having said that, and having learned to speak fluently and do business in Spanish myself (several years after and outside of my formal education), that there is no doubt that both culturally and from a business point of view, there is a huge advantage (and much pleasure derived from) having a 2nd language. The days of having to learn Italian, German, French, Korean (perhaps Japanese too) in schools I think has passed. I believe the options should be Mandarin (compulsory) and Indonesian/Spanish (2nd most spoken language in the world + growing)/Japanese being optional 3rd languages to study.

If we focus on learning the rights languages with the right systems, then I think we will all be the better for it.

Among these 12 sets of comments, a range of recurring and predictable points in public discussion – both its style and its content – are sampled. There are teacher voices and teacher-based reasoning (favouring the policy Price criticises in the case of Tracey of Melbourne, CL Angus of Richmond, James P of Melbourne and dissenting from Priorities). There are challenges to the factual basis of the programme, for example from Mat of South Melbourne, and challenges to the legitimacy of the policy-making process, from marty of frankston and FooFoo of Narnia. There is strong in-kind endorsement from WACD of Melbourne and Jack the quipper, and sarcasm and ad hominem criticisms from Ricky of Barham and Brendan of Melbourne. There are, though, also considered reorganisations of the argument and proposed new policy perspectives, exemplified by MD of Latin America.

Analysis of language policy which relies exclusively on public official texts fails to capture the shaping effects of interpretation, and reinterpretation, as shown in the small sample of public discourse just cited. Slattery, Price and the citizen bloggers represent the reception among the demos of the policy text from the state, whose authoritative voice claims the national interest and directs resources towards the problems it claims the policy will solve. The conversation opened up by these voices do more than merely dissent from or assent to, reject or embrace, the intended policy. Instead, they extend and elaborate how the core aims and the problem posed by the policy are to be understood; they refine, problematise and nuance the objectives and approaches of the policy; and they proffer alternative visions of the essential problem and strategies and purposes for its resolution.

In the debate leading up to the White Paper on Australia's place in the so-called Asian century, the dominant voices between 2009 and 2012, however, were of a different nature and intensity from the ones we have considered above, with a different set of voices prevailing. In the White Paper (essentially the report of a commissioned federal government enquiry into Australia's relations with Asia), the dominant public message as far as Asian languages were concerned was one of crisis, a crisis to which the report itself contributed. Despite declaring that all Australian students should have access to key Asian languages, it nominated three of the standard languages, Chinese, Indonesia and Japanese, but with little justification replaced Korean (which had held priority language status since 1994) with Hindi, a language practically not taught in Australian public education.

In extensive mainstream media focus on Australian–Asian relations, the prevailing voices at this time were those of business and trade officials, diplomats, politicians and think-tanks, supported by key journalists (usually writers on foreign affairs and economics), and their prominent message was one of the nation's continuing unpreparedness for a changing world. In particular, the dominant judgement of language teaching was one of overwhelming failure. These top-down messages were identical to those of their predecessors, the trade, security and diplomatic elites who in the 1980s began what became a two-decade Australian argument about the role of education in preparing for an Asian future. Both in the late 1980s and today, the demands are for overwhelming national priority to be given to 'Asia literacy', in *all* aspects of the curriculum and operation of education. The White Paper introduced the nation to a new label for the measurement of its capabilities and skills in relation to the Asian region: 'Asia capable'. As the Prime Minister's foreword expressed it:

> This White Paper is a plan to build on our strengths and shape our future. It details how, by 2025, Australia can be a winner in this Asian century by becoming more prosperous, more resilient, and sharing the new opportunities. It calls on all of us to play our part in becoming a more Asia-literate and Asia-capable nation. (Australian Government, 2012: iii)

Two facts distinguish this bout of Asia advocacy: first, essentially all the proposals have been tried before but are generally considered to have been only very marginally successful; and second, there was now the context of the global financial crisis that had begun in 2008. The financial turmoil in the euro zone combined with China's galloping economic growth had given Australia's already longstanding 'Asia project' more intensity; and Australia's sharpened reliance on commodity exports to booming China had the effect of injecting renewed urgency into discussions of Asian connections.

On 10 June 2009, all the major Australian newspapers carried stories about a report on Asian languages issued by the director of the Griffith University Asia Institute, Professor Michael Wesley (see Tomazin, 2009), calling for an investment of $11 billion in Asian language education. In Australian budgetary terms, such an amount would be truly staggering. It was calculated by the Institute as the investment required to make half the Australian population fluent in an Asian language within 30 years. While the vast scope of this claim was percolating through media discussions, a political crisis resulted in Prime Minister Rudd being overthrown by his deputy, Julia Gillard, in June 2010, and, despite claims for increased support and urgency for acquiring Asian languages skills, funding for the NALSSP was, in effect, discontinued, or 'not renewed', occasioning both lobbying to forestall its demise and trenchant criticism of it.

Greg Sheridan, prominent foreign affairs editor of *The Australian* and longstanding advocate of Asia integration and priority for Asian languages, was particularly scathing about the demise of specific budget items for Asian languages (Sheridan, 2011). On 4 June 2011 he wrote a review of a book by Michael Wesley, who had moved on to become director of the Lowy Institute (a Sydney think-tank):

> Wesley's new book, *There Goes the Neighbourhood*, is written for a general audience, and it is bold and strong ... the rise of the Asian giants is changing fundamentally Australia's international environment and this will have great consequences for us strategically, economically and culturally. (Sheridan, 2011)

He describes the mostly conventional information about the shift in economic dynamism from America and Europe to Asia, adding that the dynamic it unleashes is producing 'a world that is completely unfamiliar to us and uniquely challenging'. After lauding aspects of Wesley's book, Sheridan writes:

> Australia is not well prepared for this new and newly complex environment. The study of Asian languages apart from Chinese is falling (and even the study of Chinese in Australia is dominated by students of Chinese ethnic background).... Wesley argues convincingly that we are lazy and uninformed about Asia and, despite the presence of Asian migrants and students, we have made no significant cultural or political adjustment to the rise of our neighbours. Our foreign policy is essentially the same as it was in the 1950s. Australia is 'a nation of insular internationalists' that has continued to prosper because of a favourable global environment. We ignored the 'advice of the 1990s – that to cope with Asia, Australians need to change', but prospered anyway.

The Age, a Melbourne newspaper belonging to the Fairfax Media group, reported on 31 March 2011, under the headline 'Business in plea on Asian languages', that senior business figures had written to government and placed prominent advertisements emphasising the importance of Asian languages to Australia's economic future, amid fears that the NALSSP would be cut in the May budget (Harrison, 2011). The article cited the 'captains' of industry, 'Australian Industry Group chief executive Heather Ridout, JPMorgan chairman Sir Rod Eddington and former Business Council of Australia president Hugh Morgan', who had written a letter to federal MPs warning 'that Australia's ability to compete in Asia will suffer if the program is cut'. The evidence was that 'the world's wealth is moving to Asia – we ignore this fact at our peril', the letter said, and it went on to assert that 'We do our children a deep disservice if we fail to equip them with knowledge of the cultures and the languages of not only the fastest-growing region in the world, but the region that is on our doorstep'.

This bout of media attention to Asian language underperformance followed studies on each of the four key languages (Chinese, Indonesian, Japanese and Korean), which had concluded in 2010. Their results raised public alarm (Sturak & Naughten, 2010; Lo Bianco, 2005). A press release on 30 March 2011 from Asialink (a centre affiliated to the University of Melbourne) and the Asia Society (2011) depicted the nation as economically impaired in its ability to compete in the 'new Asian century', and implied that policy was being driven by the wrong voices, and needed to be corrected by the announced arrival of the Business Alliance for Asia Literacy. This body sent a very public letter to all government MPs, dated 16 March 2011 (and reproduced in Asialink & Asia Society, 2011) and promoted extensively in the media, whose remedy for national skill impairment was to deal not just with supply-side language planning, but the demand side too. It concluded with a call for 'significant government investment in building capacity and, importantly, demand for Asian studies and languages'.

These media reports contain the recurring features of the public discourse on Asian languages, mobilising its predictable components of the primacy of geography, economy and western decline. In its early incarnations (in the late 1980s) Australia was depicted as being too attached to its European origins and western comforts. But, after considerable success in rhetoric and funding, and yet continuing failure to produce the human subjects its lobbying demanded, this lobby had to introduce new devices. Some parties have come close to accepting English as a regular medium of exchange in Asia and have pushed instead for studies of Asian histories, societies and cultures; others have refused this and insist that public policy should encourage or oblige students to study Asian languages. Most, however, repeat past arguments, producing evidence of continuing problems with both the take-up and the outcome of language teaching programmes. In 2010 the focus turned to Indonesian, not usually characterised as a trade language, but a language of 'our closest neighbour', a powerful claim, if technically inaccurate. It was claimed by Asialink and the Asia Society (2011) that the decline in enrolments was so sharp that 'if current trends continued, there would be no students studying Indonesian at year 12 in five years'. A similar dimension has been introduced into the arguments about Chinese, one that highlights the troubled and incommensurate histories of Asia literacy and multiculturalism, captured by the claim that 'just 300 students nationally studying Chinese languages at Year 12 level ... are non-Chinese-heritage learners' (Asialink & Asia Society, 2011).

Specifically in relation to Japanese, the focus of our work here (alongside Italian), the overview report on the four language studies observed:

> after three decades of sustained and – at times rapid – growth, including six years (1994–2000) when numbers more than doubled, the student enrolment in Japanese has fallen significantly over the last six to eight years. In some sectors the level of decline in student enrolments combined with the failure to support small senior programs is close to producing a self-perpetuating cycle of decline. (Sturak & Naughten, 2010: 17)

Contained within one of the public urgings (McGregor, 2011), contrasting dawn for Asia and dark for Australian students, was the suggestion, mentioned above, which occasionally surfaces, that of favouring Asian 'studies' over languages: 'we must decide as a nation how we want to equip the next generation of Australians'. The article went to rank language skills below cultural and societal studies: 'what matters even more ... is knowledge of the people, their histories and social structures, their legal frameworks and political processes'.

The term 'Asian century' is now prominently deployed in these debates, a trope activating and seeking to naturalise a vision of inevitability and permanence. Its usage gained considerable momentum on 28 September 2011 when Prime Minister Julia Gillard announced the preparation by mid-2012 of a landmark national strategy on Australia's preparedness for 'the Asian century' (Gillard, 2011). Reciting evidence of economic growth in the region and its deep historical significance she stated:

> that is why I announce today that the Government has commissioned a White Paper on *Australia in the Asian Century*. To ask and answer the great national questions through this period of great national change.

She described the forthcoming White Paper as responding to two essential tasks, an 'intellectual task ... fully to comprehend the implications of the Asian century, fully to describe its opportunities and risks', and also a 'public task', whose aim was 'to ensure [the] implications are understood in every part of our nation'. The development of the White Paper was entrusted to the leadership of economist and public servant Dr Ken Henry, former Secretary at the Department of the Treasury, who was appointed special adviser to the Prime Minister. The issues paper produced to inform submissions and discussion in preparation of the White Paper made clear its direction, tone and purpose, continuing the theme of harnessing education and cultural life in Australia to the support of a wider agenda of regional engagement, primarily motivated by economic and strategic concerns (Australian Government, 2012; Department of Prime Minister and Cabinet, 2011).

However, on its release, one critic, Dr Benjamin Herscovitch of the Centre for Independent Studies, mounted a sustained rejection of this very assumption of a capability deficit, arguing that immigration and multiculturalism had furnished all the Asia skills the White Paper envisaged the nation needing. He said the White Paper was 'half-baked', a 'language policy gone loco' (Herscovitch, 2012a, 2013a), that it addressed a 'policy non-problem' and that it was a policy denying the reality of English in Asia (Herscovitch, 2012b, 2013b). Even longstanding supporters of Asian language policy – key diplomatic and strategic voices such as Stephen Fitzgerald (1997) – have distanced themselves from it, alongside more recent critics with trade, diplomacy and strategic planning interests (Australian Institute for International Affairs, 2013). Fitzgerald called it a 'delusion' and is cited as saying: 'I've been heavily involved [in previous Asia literacy plans] and every time, it doesn't happen. Something gets off the ground, and then it fails' (Lane, 2013a, 2013b).

We can see here the serious limits to top-down policy moves, the complexities of the relationship between public discourse and official texts on language policy. We can also find ready evidence for the deep impact of debate, discussion and argument on what constitutes language planning. It is clear that language policy, which will certainly be shaped by the White Paper, resides simultaneously in texts issued as formal announcements of language plans but also in the ways in which these plans and 'decisions' are interpreted, critiqued and debated. Public conversation, therefore, here discussed as 'interpretation', is a critical component of language policy-making. That is, the intention of policy in texts rides closely with its interpretation in public discussion. Implementation, and personal language behaviour, the third crucial element, is the subject of our research.

Prime Ministerial Visions for New Australias

Language policy in Australia has long aimed to remake the nation. This overarching meta-policy shaping the specific content of language policies is apparent in the social visions of national purpose associated with the Prime Minister of the day.

Prior to Rudd's China-centred Asianism (Callick, 2011), all Prime Ministers can be associated with a cultural-linguistic label in this way. We can trace this pattern from the historic turning point represented by the 1972 federal election, which marked the end of almost a quarter of a century of conservative government. This claim to a 'historic turning point' is due to the depth of social and cultural change initiated by the election of Gough Whitlam of the Australian Labour Party as the 21st Prime Minister. Although his government was short-lived (1972–75), its language policy legacy is substantial, as it initiated the first support for community languages, as well as programmes in Aboriginal bilingual education. Whitlam's period in office also represents the formal beginning and adoption of multiculturalism as public policy. In the context of the Vietnam War and Australia's insistence on an independent foreign policy, that government's repudiation of dependence on the United States and Britain is perhaps best labelled 'Australianism'.

Whitlam was defeated by Malcolm Fraser of the Liberal–National Party Coalition, who served as 22nd Prime Minister, from 1975 to 1983. In several respects Fraser was the most significant leader on policies of cultural pluralism. He commissioned the Galbally report of 1978, famous for making multiculturalism a bipartisan policy and initiating a large number of programmes of support for language education (Galbally, 1978). In 1982 he initiated the Senate Standing Committee on Education and the Arts to enquire into the possibility of devising a national language policy. Fraser's ideology reflected a kind of cultural multiculturalism, in that while he was active in recognising diversity in public policy and institutionalising it, he was also keen to remove class elements in interpreting multiculturalism, a legacy of the trade union basis of Labour politics under Whitlam. Fraser's approach stressed culture, rather than how social class and ethnic cultures overlapped, and his approach was to celebrate and affirm cultural differences within an overarching national unity, rather than analysing the occupational or class inequalities between different cultural groups in workplaces or schools.

Robert J. (Bob) Hawke of the Australian Labour Party defeated Fraser and served as the 23rd Prime Minister, from 1983 to 1991. Hawke in office returned the emphasis in multicultural policy back to issues of inequality and social class. He continued the national language policy enquiry initiated by Fraser and steered the adoption of Australia's first formal national language policy, the 1987 National Policy on Languages (NPL) (Lo Bianco, 1987). Many new programmes in Asian studies and languages commenced within the comprehensive approach adopted by the NPL, rather than as separate policy items. (It was under the NPL that Japanese came to replace French as the most widely taught language at secondary school, with Italian securing first position in primary school, the two languages that were of interest in the study reported in this volume.) This integrated approach, however, was dismantled under the Prime Ministership of Paul Keating, also of the Labour Party, who overthrew Hawke in an internal political shift and served as 24th Prime Minister, from 1991 to 1996. Under Keating's steward-ship, with a strong role played by his Education Minister John Dawkins, the NPL was dissolved and replaced by a new statement, the Australian Language and Literacy Policy (ALLP) (Dawkins, 1991). Rather than the government-wide comprehensive language approach of the NPL, the ALLP concentrated only on the education sphere. Within this, it ranked Asian languages and English above all other language interests, including heritage or community languages and other European languages. However, this too was soon dismantled by Keating, when, in collaboration with the state government of Queensland, in which Kevin Rudd was Cabinet Secretary, he moved for the adoption of the NALSAS report (Rudd, 1995). The resulting well funded policy was notable for its exclusive ranking of four languages (Chinese, Indonesian, Japanese and Korean) above all others, explicitly selected on trade and security terms. This accommodation was initially continued by the restored conservative government under Prime Minister John Howard, leading the Liberal–National Coalition, who served as 25th Prime Minister, from 1996 to 2007. However, over time Howard came to stress English literacy in debates about language education, and facilitated the emergence of an English-based commercialisation of higher education. His government promoted Australia as a location both for the study of English as a foreign language in short courses and for English-medium higher education, effectively producing a vast expansion in the numbers of international students in Australian education. His government ultimately terminated the NALSAS programme in 2002, two years short of its intended completion date.

These successive visions encapsulate how language policy and its related cultural dimensions have contributed to cultural, economic and social life in Australia. They have tended to be far more than simply how language policy reflects society, but how language policy can foster renewal and change. We can summarise them in the following terms.

- Whitlam promoted a class-based multiculturalism, with a strong 'Australianist' focus (i.e. distancing both Britain and the United States in seeking an independent foreign policy aware of its cultural conse-quences).
- Fraser embraced much of the spirit of Australian independence in external affairs, though he was closer to Australia's traditional allies, but in domestic policy his moves were more radical and extensive. He downplayed questions of inequality in language and cultural policy but

much more strongly pursued policies in recognition of cultural diversity.

- Hawke returned policy-making to a broadly Whitlam-like stance, with a strong emphasis in language policy on immigrant and Aboriginal opportunity, supporting English as a second language and the rights of those whose mother tongue was not English.
- Within his own political party Keating replaced class multiculturalism with Asianism – a strong emphasis on a new vision for Australia as an integral part of the Asian region and stressing the educational and language consequences of this. His alliance with Rudd led to explicit priority for Asian languages.
- Howard's guiding philosophy on diversity was to stress the assimilation of minorities into an Anglo-nationalism. His external ties were with the Anglosphere nations of tradition (Britain) and alliance (the United States). He had a strong focus on English-medium education and on a commercialised industry of English teaching, and so the touchstones of his period in office were promotion of commerce through English, an emphasis on literacy in education over English as a second language, and stressing cultural assimilation to mainstream values for minorities.

Kevin Rudd restored the Australian Labour Party to government in late 2007 but served only a short period as 26th Prime Minister, to mid-2010. He returned language policy to his vision of Australia making its way under a China-centred Asianism and his main language education move was the establishment of the NALSSP, emphasising the same four languages of trade, commerce and strategic relations: Chinese, Indonesian, Japanese and Korean. However, as Keating replaced Hawke in an internal party political reorganisation in 1991, so was Rudd replaced in an internal Labour Party political struggle by his deputy, Julia Gillard, at the time of writing serving as 27th Prime Minister. In Gillard's political career language issues had never been a feature, and until the 2012 White Paper no coherent vision of language and cultural ideology had emerged under her premiership. However, during her period as federal Minister for Education she had issued policy in support of adult literacy, using arguments about employment and social progress, and so emphasising some of the Whitlam/Hawke class-based approach to language and literacy policy. Her commissioning of the White Paper on Australia in the Asian century, and the defence of its implementation, suggested that her Prime Ministership would be associated with this particular socio-cultural vision for the nation. As Minister for Education, she had implicitly supported the dismantling or weakening of the Indigenous languages component of Aboriginal bilingual education, but she has made few (if any) other remarks on language education or its purposes.

This sequence of cultural ideologies and national visions reveals an energetic if contested project of national reconstruction. It is distinctively Australian because the interplay of historical inheritance (European institutions, culture and politico-legal structures) is enveloped within an Asian geo-political and security framework that no other Anglophone nation has experienced. The policy arenas in which this national project of cultural reconstruction has been played out include Indigenous affairs, British connections, American ties, Asian geography and an initially European and then a later globally sourced multiculturalism. Language education policy has been a key site of this deep social transformation.

Visioning and agitating

A remarkable exercise in national visioning under direct Prime Ministerial guidance occurred shortly after Rudd's election. In an explicit exercise in charting a new pattern of national identity and practical political action the Prime Minister convened the Australia 2020 Summit, 19–20 April 2008 (Commonwealth of Australia, 2008). Participants were selected on the basis of invitations and nominations. Rudd's election victory had been emphatic and emphatic was the exercise in remaking the direction and fortunes of the 'lucky country'. Operating like a hands-on workshop, with its invited members representing various social formations and interest groups, with preparatory summits for schools and other groups, culminating in the convention of the 1000 'best and brightest', all supplied with reading material and posing the key questions of social policy, regional integration and economic renewal, in which Indigenous and Asian issues featured prominently, but multiculturalism was downplayed (Australia 2020, 2008).

Everything about the organisation, publicity, texts and prose of the activity stressed reconstruction, sweeping away the Howard policies and the Howard ethos, and making a new nation. Opponents excoriated the idea as vain, pompous and unrealistic and its agenda as transparent and socialist (e.g. Roskam, 2008). Supporters relished the consultation and the apparently open waters in which to set sail the national ship, and imagined a new and more inclusive destination. Many positions resided in between, but no one could foresee both how futile and how short-lived the vast vision exercise would prove to be. What follows is an extracted account from the preparatory documents and the concluding report (Australia 2020, 2008), looking only at languages, their associations and meaning.

The themes of the summit themselves suggested and organised how languages were regarded. These were: The productivity agenda; The future of the Australian economy; Population, sustainability, climate change, water and the future of our cities; Future directions for rural industries and rural communities; A long-term national health strategy; Strengthening communities, supporting families and social inclusion; Options for the future of Indigenous Australia; Towards a creative Australia; The future of Australian governance; and Australia's future security and prosperity in a rapidly changing region and world.

Leaving aside mentions of 'language' that refer essentially to discourse, such as calls for a new constitution to use more inclusive language – 'The Constitution needs to be rewritten and reworked so it is intelligible. The language should be lyrical and needs to say what it means and mean what it says' (Australia 2020, 2008: 318) – or for policy to be more comprehensible, there were essentially three categories of mention for languages: Indigenous, immigrant (though rarely called this) and Asian-foreign.

The themes and this classification were in fact prefigured in the preparatory material, which subtly and not-so-subtly guided the organisation of and orientation to problems and ideas of the summit. It is relevant to consider briefly how languages, their purposes and place, were positioned and how the outcomes produced were manufactured by the process. The preamble of the preparatory material (Australia 2020, 2008) recounted shifts in global power, and in particular the emergence of the economies of China and India, with their growth exercising a 'gravitational pull on surrounding countries'; Australia was positioned as being advantaged in these new arrangements but requiring the nation to develop 'international literacy'. This new kind of literacy would be bolstered by the number and origin of inbound foreign students and the claimed 'decline' in English as a first language. An instance of tendentious prose argued that:

> with the growth in population in Asia and Africa, the proportion of people speaking English as a first language will reduce. It is estimated that approximately two-thirds of the world's population will not speak English as a first language by 2050.

The internet was claimed to be 'now multilingual' but, despite this,

> 85 per cent of Australian students graduate from Year 12 without a second language. Indonesia is one of our closest neighbours and an important regional partner, however only 15 full-time academics now work on Indonesia across Australia. Only 2.9% of tertiary students study Asia-related subjects and in 2006 only 400 university students enrolled to study Indonesian.

Other evidence was supplied of decline in language study, restrictions in language availability and general deterioration in the national language effort.

Countering this was a collection of national advantages, such as Australia's 'unique geographic location, large educated and multicultural population, and Australians across the globe'. A series of policy questions were posed, aimed at channelling thinking towards regional engagement, institutional structures for collaboration across the Asia Pacific and a characterisation of Australians as potentially well, but actually poorly, prepared for the momentous changes enveloping the world, all tied to key ideas of prosperity, security and participation.

In the final document from the Summit, containing reports from syndicate groups tasked with addressing the themes mentioned above, the vast majority of specific references to languages were tied to Asia and 'Asia literacy' (sometimes 'regional literacy' or 'international literacy'). Every specific mention of a category of languages related to 'Asia' or 'Indigenous'. Immigrant languages were rarely tied to education, culture or commerce, but were instead linked to welfare, immigrant integration or various kinds of symbolic inclusion. Immigrant languages were constituted as advantageous for domestic purposes and limited aims, but even here only Asian ones were mentioned. Indigenous languages were invariably constituted as heritage, occasionally tied to successful or intact cultural maintenance for Indigenous groups, or to symbols of national unity or identity. Asian languages were constituted as essentially foreign, and in the service not of civilisation, or even knowledge in a more or less cultural sense, but instrumentally, as tools in facilitating Australian economic and security purposes in the region. There was no association of European or world languages with commerce or Australian futures in any more or less internationalist way and no mention of multicultural aims other than those which service internationalism.

The 399-page report concluded with a series of 'By 2020' declarations. For example

By 2020 Asian studies and the teaching of Asian languages will be commonplace. (p. 396)

[B]y 2020 Australia should be a republic with a female Prime Minister of non-Anglo extraction, a bridge between East Asia and the declining west and a country trusted and accepted as part of Asia. There should be seamless interaction between Australia and the Asian region, its cultures and languages. (p. 399)

[B]y 2020, a key goal will be a national strategy for Australia's place in Asia covering our identity, Asia literacy and membership of regional bodies. Policy should be geared for Asian engagement through absorption of Asia literacy into the national psyche, including funded programs and investments in language, culture and education. Every student from kindergarten to year 12 should be fluent in an Asian language. (p. 399)

In language planning terms the 2020 Summit represents a combination of public debate, directed, guided and even manufactured to some extent, and the display of personal commitment behaviours and displays of fealty to the correct national models.

The reports and other documents of the Summit are not official texts in the sense used here, since they remain as recommendations, and have been largely overtaken by subsequent events; however, they are an important example of the effort of guiding language policy and of naturalising certain ways in which to organise the field of interest and favour particular outcomes. Influencing policy requires being admitted to policy-making conversations, but, despite the favourable conditions that support all the language policy goals of the Summiteers, how can we explain the ongoing crisis of Asian language teaching? Extensive funding has been provided for Asian language education, far beyond what any other category of languages has received, for more than 25 years, and yet, within just two years of the optimism and enthusiasm of the Summit, with the Prime Minister of the country a major and direct champion of Asian language teaching and with targeted funding and supportive mainstream media, and low or sporadic opposition, the worst had happened.

In May 2010 the federal government issued its four separate reports documenting the fortunes of Chinese, Indonesian, Japanese and Korean, reproducing the language-specific documentation approach of the National Languages and Literacy Institute of Australia in the early 1990s. The conclusions were devastating, at least according to a consolidation of the four studies issued by the Asia Education Foundation (AEF), based at the University of Melbourne (AEF, 2010a), dramatically expressed in its accompanying press release of 26 May entitled: 'Asian languages education crisis deepens' (AEF, 2010b). The announcement of the findings of the four research studies was introduced as follows: 'the state of Australia's Asian languages education is far worse than feared and continuing to decline'. The press release went on to warn that the aspiration in the NALSSP 'to double the number of Year 12 students fluent in an Asian language by 2020 faces huge challenges unless there is attitudinal change across the Australian community'.

Needless to say 'attitudinal change across the Australian community' is what, colloquially, might be called 'a big ask'. What, then, is the problem? Since the policy texts at the level of intention are clear and unambiguous, relatively well supported, and since the policy discourses and debates are overwhelmingly favourable, and the level of interpretation is supportive and coherent with the policy texts, where can we look to identify the failure of language planning that can help explain, and rectify, the problem of Asian language teaching? What, also, is the place of languages other than Asian ones? For what purposes should they be studied, by which students and in which institutions?

Italian and Japanese

In this volume we try to offer some answers to these important questions by looking at the ambitions, history and nature of Australian language policy through a focus on two languages – Italian and Japanese. These two exemplify two clear periods, traditions and histories in Australian language policy-making. While each has its distinct sociology and its particular psychological reality, both also have a representative quality.

Italian is perceived in public discussion as not just Italian, but as representative of two other traditions or categories of Australian language education: first, the phase of community (heritage) language teaching, which is an essentially bottom-up experience of language planning beginning in the mid-1970s and still present today, even if in attenuated form; and second, the category of 'European languages', which, by contrast, is the historical experience of top-down language choice, best represented by French and German. Among community languages Italian is perhaps the 'classic', the one most successfully included in public education, becoming the second most widely taught language in the country, exceeding French and German in the European language category, from which, for most of Australia's history of compulsory education, it was entirely absent.

Japanese is perceived in public discussion as not just Japanese, but as representative of the category of 'trade' languages and 'Asian' languages, that is, of the pragmatic reasoning that has sustained language planning in Australia since the late 1980s. It is also deeply representative of the political project of Asian 'regionalism' now becoming reinvented as adaptation to the 'Asian century'. Since 1990, that is, even before the adoption (in 1995) of the Rudd report (COAG, 1994) on Asian language teaching, Japanese has been the most widely taught language in the country.

On the basis of this discussion, we aim to throw some light on the problems of language policy attainments and push forward thinking in the field of language education planning, for it seems that, even having all the favourable conditions for the making of language policies, their outcomes will not satisfy those engaged in agitation and visioning 'unless there is attitudinal change…'.

Notes

1. Year 12 has iconic significance in Australian education discussions. It is the final year of schooling, though not the final year of compulsory education, which is year 10. Well over three-quarters of students complete 12 years of schooling; retention and success at year 12 tend to be discussed as proxy measures of school success, in terms of the transition to the labour market or to higher education, especially university.
2. VCE is the Victorian Certificate of Education, a credential applied to the final two years of schooling, years 11 and 12, in the state of Victoria.

2   Australia's Italian and Japanese

Reprise

The discussion in the previous chapter traversed the wide terrain of the relations between the forms in which language policy is produced. We argued that it is a mistake to view language policy just as what is announced in official texts, and tried to show how policy is shaped also in discussion, public debate and generally in discourse. The text of policy on languages usually represents the intentions of people in official domains, their decisions on what is to be taught in schools, whereas the ensuing discussion/debate modifies or refines and generally interprets policy and sometimes subverts and changes it. We also looked briefly at English and the Anglosphere and some thinking about the role of English in the world; the position of English is relevant to the extent that it influences the attitudes people might hold of how much effort in schools should be expended on languages in addition to English.

In Chapter 1 we also discussed the context of politics and power in Australia, and outlined the visions successive Prime Ministers have had about cultural and language issues, focusing on those who have governed Australia since the 1970s, when language became a regular concern of the policy scene. This process of Prime Ministerial 'visioning' led to an energetic commitment to Asian language teaching to facilitate trade and geo-political security arrangements in the region, and this purpose for language policy is the one that prevails in both discussion (interpretation) and intention (official policy). However, it was noted that, at the time of writing, Australia had not one but three official language policy statements at the federal level. By contrast, at the *national* level, meaning the coordinated effort of eight state, territory and federal governments, Australia is on the verge of promulgating its first national curriculum for schools. This allocates a secure and fixed place to languages. Chinese and Italian have been the first two to be prepared, but there is no limit to the number which may eventually be included.

It was noted that the three language policies extant at the federal government level partially contradict each other, prioritise different languages and different reasons for teaching languages, and appear to support a much more complex idea of the functions of language policy texts. Official texts do not just 'announce' language policy: they also serve symbolic functions of 'standing for' certain interests or ideas, and political functions of placating certain interests. To ascertain what really is intended in language policy, an analysis of the process of their interpretation is critical. Official texts are also expressed in a form that suggests more the meta policy, or national ideology, that structures them, such as we find in the Prime Ministerial visions. Their interpretation at school and district level is, then, partly a process of translation of the policy for the context and process of implementation.

We also looked at how the prioritisation of Asian languages, specifically the national and official languages of Australia's main trading partners, has yielded mixed results. In fact, key advocates for Asian languages register disappointment and even alarm at the outcomes. Why, after more than two decades of priority, extensive funding, absence of systematic opposition and championing at the highest levels of government is it possible today to describe Asian language planning as being in a deepening 'crisis'? Partly this will be the language of agitation for resources, partly it will be a reflection of systemic issues, and partly it will be, as the advocates claim, to do with prevailing 'attitudes'. To probe whether there is indeed a crisis, and in what ways it could be remedied, the analysis has to be broadened; that is, the vision of what constitutes language policy will have to expand further, which is why our notion of 'language planning policy' includes policy implementation, that is, teaching and learning. In turn, implementation includes attitudinal and cultural factors alongside that practical activity – what participants think and believe, and what values they hold, in addition to the actual practices of teaching and learning, within an overall ecology of communication policy.

Implementation therefore needs to be rescued conceptually from a narrow understanding of it as simply putting into action what others have decided, of enacting received intentions (and, as we argue, those intentions will in any case have already been modified by the interpretation phase of discussion and debate). Implementation will have to be conceived as a more active and agentive space.

This chapter commences our review of this third aspect of language education policy, the space of implementation, and begins to describe the protagonists of implementation, mainly but not exclusively teachers and learners, and the roles they perform in the enactment (interpretation, and indeed 'constituting') of language education policy. The languages in question are Australia's two most widely taught languages, Italian and Japanese, each representing a key phase of the history of visions of cultural and language renewal in Australia since the 1970s.

Who Studies Which Languages?

We will begin by addressing the question of who studies languages and which languages they study.

Unfortunately, any account of school provision is complicated by the highly devolved nature of Australian education. Essentially it is run by some 30 education jurisdictions. Further, about one-third of students attend non-government (independent and Catholic) schools. Lo Bianco and Slaughter (2009) reported that a total 1,401,550 students were enrolled in languages; in aggregate terms Italian and Japanese accounted for almost half of these enrolments (Table 2.1). These figures represent the most complete data presently available across the primary and secondary cycles of schooling and in all education jurisdictions. Table 2.2 shows the main languages offered in the primary cycle of education and Table 2.3 those offered in the secondary cycle.

In this overview of the national language scene there is a consistent group of six languages that make up the bulk of the language learning effort in Australia today, but these figures conceal the fact that the total number of languages taught is much larger: 47 are taught and examined in some part of the education sector.

Table 2.1 Student enrolments in languages in primary and secondary schools in Australia, 2006

Language	Student numbers
Japanese	332,943
Italian	322,023
Indonesian	209,939
French	207,235
German	126,920
Chinese (Mandarin)	81,358
Arabic	25,449
Spanish	20,518
Total	1,326,385

Table 2.2 Students enrolments in languages in primary schools (years 1, 3 and 6) in Australia, 2006

	Year 1	Year 3	Year 6	Totals
Italian	22,521	32,652	35,446	218,301
Japanese	12,867	21,920	45,890	176,245
Indonesian	9,942	19,537	26,273	131,245
French				69,718
German				57,604
Chinese (Mandarin)				48,405

Table 2.3 Students enrolments in languages in secondary schools (years 7, 10, 11 and 12) in Australia, 2006

	Year 7	Year 10	Year 11	Year 12	Totals
Japanese	63,272	11,430	5,627	4,667	84,996
French	45,085	11,543	6,353	4,607	67,588
Italian	35,449	8,172	3,895	2,740	50,256
German					2,147
Indonesian					1,618

The main six in descending order of representation are Japanese, Italian, Indonesian, French, German and Chinese (Mandarin). The internal differentiations show that Japanese is strongly present at both secondary and primary levels, while Italian is stronger at primary than at secondary. French is stronger at secondary. Japanese and Italian together represent almost 50% of total enrolments, and with the inclusion of Indonesian and French the total reaches 81%. Adding German and Chinese brings the total to 97%.

In public debate on language questions there is often reference to the need to teach fewer languages, and complaints that students are not offered consistent teaching of one language, or that students are unable to complete a programme of study in a single language.

Geography, economy, demography

The list of languages discussed above reflects crucial phases of Australian education and its response to how three factors have been debated in public life: geography, economy and demography.

Australia's post-war immigration was subject to a national policy of population boosting, an important characteristic that shapes how language policy and cultural policy have evolved and how they are understood today (Jupp, 2007). The 'new population' was recruited through the direct action of the Australian government, with a clear intention to produce a larger domestic market and to reduce the territorial vulnerability exposed by Japanese bombing of the northern city of Darwin and penetration of Sydney Harbour with midget submarines during the Second World War. These two incidents are part of a longer story of perceived vulnerability that Australians have felt, as an island outpost of the British Empire at the edge of the Asian landmass.

The post-war migration programme fundamentally changed the nature of Australian civic life. Migrants were recruited as permanent 'new Australians', with the express aim that they would become settler citizens and the cultural aim that they would assimilate, learn English and generally lose their differences. The literature on this experience is extensive (Koleth, 2010) and its broadest themes show how Australia changed despite intending initially to refuse such change, culturally, religiously and ethnically.

The impact of this immigration has been spatially differentiated. Since much of the programme concerned the recruitment of a labour force, more industrialised areas, such as the large cities (Melbourne and Sydney) and the industrial areas of smaller cities (Adelaide and Perth), tended to receive more immigrants, in reception area suburbs. Consequently, the character of these cities and their distribution of languages, religions and ethnicities have been shaped directly by immigration (Burnley, 2001). The language policy effects of settlement history are also evident, since it was in Melbourne and Adelaide that multicultural policies began and there also, along with Sydney, that the adoption of a specific range of languages in the education and health services and public administration was pioneered (Koleth, 2010). Subsequently, residential and social (occupational) mobility for the immigrant communities was facilitated by their acquisition of English (Burnley, 2001). Pragmatism in language policy-making led to the creation of what for a long time was the world's largest language settlement initiative, the Adult Migrant Education Program, from as early as the late 1940s (Martin, 1998).

The importation of a labour force changed the public sphere in large part because of the Australian institution of compulsory voting. Since the law required all citizens to vote and new arrivals rapidly acquired citizenship on completion of residency requirements (Chesterman & Galligan, 1999), issues of migrant absorption and the demands of migrants themselves, or of the more integrated English-speaking second generation, were placed on the public agenda. This was the mechanism whereby in the early to mid-1970s Australian governments responded to the presence of immigrant populations, and a distinctively Australian multicultural politics and policy were forged (Jupp, 2007; Koleth, 2010).

Enter Italian and Japanese

Italian-speaking immigrants were for much of the post-war period the largest single category apart from British new arrivals, reaching 916,100 or 4.6% of the national population in 2011 (ABS Ancestry, 2013). In the 2001 census (Khoo & Lucas, 2004), Italian ancestry remains the largest grouping after 'Australian', 'English' and 'Irish', at 800,256, a 29% increase between 1986 and 2001. Of this number a relatively high 78.9% have Australian citizenship. They are concentrated in regions of initial settlement, highest in the state of Victoria, which has considerably higher proportions of Italians, Greeks and others of southern European backgrounds compared with all other regions, contrasted with Tasmania, a principally rural and non-industrial state, which has the lowest proportion.

Persons of Japanese ancestry counted 31,433 in 2001, a 125% increase from 1986, and they had the lowest rate of Australian citizenship of sampled groups, at 19% (Khoo & Lucas, 2004: 35), possibly influenced by Japanese law linking citizenship to ancestry, but also by the professional status of many. In 2006, 40,968 declared Japanese ancestry.

A comparison of the Italian and Japanese languages in Australian schooling (Lo Bianco, 2003) shows their different histories, each entering school and university education relatively late, for different reasons and now reflecting distinctive sociologies. Italian first entered in a minor key as a language of western cultural prestige, Japanese as a language of Asian cultural prestige. Their domination in terms of enrolment numbers is a later circumstance. Italian's initial cultural prestige, its elevated presence, was overwhelmed by its presence on the streets, its community or demotic appearance as a language of immigration and of immigrants. It then became a language of the community, actively spoken and sustaining newspaper, radio and television audiences. For this reason the usage of the increasingly popular American designation 'heritage language' fails to capture the dual character of languages like Italian in Australia, which is learned by those of Italian ancestry for 'heritage' reasons, but also by others of non-Italian heritage for 'community' reasons and by both groups for reasons of 'cultural prestige'. Because it is actively spoken, the 'recovery' ethos that characterises some heritage language communities does not apply, or does so only partially. Similarly, the initial prestige of Japanese, its elevated presence, was overwhelmed by its presence in commercial, trade and tourism contexts.

The spoken presence of Italian in 'the streets' and the spoken presence of Japanese in 'the boardrooms and resorts' of Australian cities and rural areas persuaded education planners that there was a practical case for the teaching of both. This transformed their purposes, since languages of

cultural prestige are invariably taught to facilitate access to works of literature, whereas languages taught because of the presence of communities
of speakers, their institutions and organisations, are taught to facilitate
conversations and interactions with actual speakers.

The main encounter between Australia, Australians and Australian
education with Italian was related to its contribution to the transformation
of urban Australia cultural life under multiculturalism. For Japanese, the
main encounter was in its contribution to the economic transformation
of Australia, and its later contribution to cultural life in Australia's cities.
These shifts and changes are deep and have lasted several decades in each
case. The figures presented above show that Italian and Japanese remain
the most diffused languages in the education system, and appear to reflect
a compromise, a kind of formula that educators have forged with staff in
schools to include one European and one Asian language. In many cases this
is Indonesian and French, or German and Chinese, but there are innumer-
able other permutations.

The place of Italian

As we saw in Chapter 1, however, the preference in Australian education
planning is clearly on Asia, with priority attention in discourse and in policy
texts. The first of the three reviewed policies in Chapter 1, the National
Statement and Plan for Languages, which includes Italian, is significantly
less important in policy and politics than the third, the National Asian
Languages and Studies in Schools Program (NALSSP), which does not. So
what is the reality of Italian today in Australia? What can its future role be
in the context of a Europeanising Italy and an Asianising Australia? Some
insight can be gained from Canada, where lobbying for Italian has gone
through similar steps and stages and makes almost identical claims. These
include its local presence, bilateral trade and a roll call of claims to cultural
prestige, with a final link to humanistic claims for a liberal education,
leavened with a nod to commerce.

Why study Italian, asks the Department of Hispanic and Italian studies,
University of Victoria in British Columbia.

> As more Canadians speak Italian than any other language in Canada after
> English and French, and as Italy has become an increasingly important
> trading partner with Canada, career opportunities exist in the fields of
> teaching ... translation, business ... design, fashion, hotel management
> and the travel industry. An understanding of the language and culture
> of Italy is essential for a greater appreciation of such celebrated figures

in Western civilization as Dante, Petrarch, Leonardo da Vinci, Michelangelo, Machiavelli, Galileo, Vivaldi, Verdi, Pirandello, and Fellini. Italy has been a principal contributor to the evolution of the arts, sciences, and ideas for the greater part of the last 700 years. Therefore, knowledge of the Italian language is an invaluable tool for acquiring a truly complete liberal education. Nowadays such an education is becoming a desirable prerequisite for employment by the business community. (http://web.uvic.ca/hispanital/home/index.htm)

Here we see a mirror image of the discourse of justification for Italian in Australia: the common 'other' language (after English and French in Canada, English in Australia), the commercial and the cultural. The same discourse appears in Australia.

However, time takes its toll, steadily transferring claims for an Italian birthplace to the ancestry column, converting the 'mother tongue' into the 'grandmother tongue'. For the 2011 census the Australian Bureau of Statistics listed 10 languages for which assistance in census completion would be offered; despite being the first and second most claimed language in four states and not lower than the fifth in any, Italian was omitted from the list. First generation Italian monolingualism had become second-generation bilingualism, or even third-generation English monolingualism in many cases. This provides a measure of the changing status of Italian in Australia, its journey from community to heritage language. While Italian might remain a widely spoken community language, language shift and intergenerational loss are gathering pace.

As the language is transmitted less and less within homes and families, it depends more and more on transmission within education. But here we find a double meaning in the idea of 'heritage' language. Writing in the journal *Arts and Humanities in Higher Education*, David Moss traces three phases of Italian's presence in Australian formal education, especially in universities. he labels these phases 'Skyhooks to the sacred, 1929–1963', 'Moored to multiculturalism, 1963–1988' and 'Unhooked and unmoored, 1988–2002'. 'Italianists in Australian universities' (Moss, 2004: 127) have drawn on the canonical claims of Italian civilisation, for which Moss cites an observation made by Peter Nichols: 'culturally, we are all Italy's children' (Nichols, 1973: 27); they have also drawn on the physical, local and 'ordinary' presence of the Italian language in Australia, spoken by Italians, Italo-Australians and non-Italian Australians who have learned Italian.

Here the 'heritage' argument has two kinds of presence: first, as a classical (civilisational and shared) heritage; and second, as a living and current heritage. It is clear that these are very different entities: the classical heritage resides mostly within academic disciplines located in arts and humanities programmes in universities (Goad, 2004); the lived and current heritage resides in primary school programmes of language maintenance. These are not even remotely similar, but their dual presence has served to maintain Italian in Australian education, and supports Moss's analysis that the classicist presence (canonical literature, art history etc.) that constitutes Italianist studies has 'protected' the language from contemporary experience (a 'contemporary' experience of a nation under considerable stress) and its peasant and working-class presence in the Australian community, sourced from mass migration, itself caused by national duress.

One of the functions of heritage is to mark the past; this was shown in the visit by the Governor-General of Australia, Quentin Bryce, to Italy for the marking in 2011 of the 150th anniversary of the unification of Italy and to express gratitude for Italian donations to support the Queensland flood victims that year. The following tells this tale, in cultural and international relations terms, about contemporary Italy and Italian heritage in Australia, and about the mediating populations, the Italian Australians and Australians in Italy.

Conzano and Ingham

The website of Conzano, a small town in the north Italian region of Piedmont, reports Bryce's visit on 5 June 2011. The community celebrations to mark her visit took place in Piazza Australia, the main municipal square, named in 1992 in honour of the mass migration of Conzano's citizens to the equally small town of Ingham in the far north of Queensland (Douglas, 1994). In Piazza Australia, Bryce unveiled a plaque in memory of Giuseppe (Joe) Cantamessa. After migrating in 1907 Cantamessa became a labour activist, introducing innovations into cane cultivation and harvesting technologies, and performed many social and political roles such as campaigning against the British Preference League, which discriminated against non-British cane-cutters and led to safety and accident prevention campaigns to reduce the many deaths among cane-cutters. Although naturalised in 1913 Cantamessa had to endure vilification and eventually internment for three and a half years (Elkner et al., 2005).

The mayor's welcome speech for the Governor-General described Conzano migration as an inter-oceanic exodus from the European Alps to tropical sugar cane farms, an exodus which commenced in 1891. The mayor expressed pride that Conzano was the only Italian municipality to dedicate its principal piazza to Australia and unveiled the work of a local artist featuring a kangaroo. A local street name recalls Ingham, just like a square in Ingham names Conzano and a street in the national capital of Canberra recalls Joe Cantamessa. Mutual naming has the effect of bringing distant realities closer and forging a micro-communication community, a 'we' form of talk for an experience across space and time.

The specific immigration narrative is the familiar one: peasant farmers move vast distances and exchange familiarity for strangeness in the interests of material betterment for their families, but who through metaphor and effort of will make society and culture converge. Cutting sugarcane in a distant and different land, the mayor suggested, is just a version of pruning vines in a close and familiar land. It is the work that workers do for their families, and it is honest and decent. Language forms these bonds and symbolises them too. The mayor noted that many Ingham 'citizens of British origin', through shared cutting of cane, learned something of 'our Conzanese dialect'. The mayor recalled that work is more than mere labour, it is exchange and interaction, epitomised by the life of Cantamessa.

In these speeches and encounters standard Italian, Conzanese and English, code-switching forms part of a ritualised encounter, words peppering a discourse to mark connection, past encounter and shared experience, but also underscoring the language shift that has occurred, that hardship was endured and permanent relations established.

The Australian Embassy in Rome produces a regular newsletter, whose 4 July 2011 issue (Australian Embassy, 2011) reproduced the steps of the Governor-General's visit, and a text box noted that 'more than 850,000 Australians claim Italian ancestry'. The Governor-General's itinerary perfectly summarises the Italian–Australian connection today, overwhelmingly dedicated to acts of remembrance, leavened by culture (visiting the Australian pavilion at the Venice Biennale), security and memorialisation (laying a wreath in Sicily to commemorate Australian airmen killed in the Sicily campaign of the Second World War), but also scientific, sporting, economic and cultural relations and activities, and 'Catholic' activities (the official papal audience, an Indigenous Australian arts exhibition, 'Rituals of Life', in the Vatican museums, the opening of Domus Australia, a pilgrimage centre that achieved promotion during the canonisation of Australia's first Catholic saint, Mary Mackillop, in 2010).

The place of Japanese

The profile of Japanese migration to, and presence in, Australia is radically different from that of Italian migration. Until the Meiji Ishin period from 1868 (Jansen, 2000), sometimes controversially called the Meiji Restoration, Japanese policy banned migration abroad, and in fact it was a capital offence for Japanese people to leave the country (Sissons, 2001).

The Meiji Ishin was essentially a complicated national reconstruction that dramatically changed the political structures of the country, ushered in by the ending of Edo period (late Tokugawa Shogunate) and the restoration of imperial rule in 1868. The Meiji Ishin was directly shaped by American intrusion into Japanese affairs to force the isolated country to open up to trade, and the industrialisation and modernisation which followed led to both major internal population displacements and to foreign migration.

As Japan proceeded to assimilate western ideas and technology, it emerged from a long period of isolation only to confront the growing presence of Tsarist imperial Russia in neighbouring territories. Japan's isolation coincided with restrictions on Australian immigration. These applied to many nationalities and groups of people, including Japanese, and as a result only 30 Japanese had settled in Victoria by 1891 (Immigration Museum, 2011) whereas more 1242 passports were issued to Japanese people travelling to Australia in 1893 and 1128 in 1898 (Sissons, 2001). The key industry was pearling and the culturing of pearls. The pearling centre of Broome in the Kimberley region of Western Australia has the most extensively documented history of the Japanese presence in Australia through migration, but there was also a presence in the Torres Strait Islands, located between Queensland and Papua New Guinea, where pearlers introduced and adapted their Japanese techniques for culturing pearls.

On 1 January 1901, the Commonwealth of Australia was proclaimed, in which the existing British colonies, New South Wales, Victoria, Queensland, South Australia, Western Australia and Tasmania, formed a single federal state. Although some temporary admissions were allowed in the immediate post-federation period, and despite some relaxation of immigration requirements, for example exempting Japanese from the notorious dictation test, an instrument used to keep out unwanted immigrants, the numbers of Japanese remained small. By the 1911 census the occupational profile of Japanese immigrants showed that the vast bulk were still engaged in various aspects of the pearling industry, although with significant numbers working in sugar cultivation in northern Queensland, so that by the second decade after federation almost 90% of Australia's resident Japanese were located in Queensland. As with the bulk of immigration, there were many more males than females, necessitating intermarriage or return home, or the bringing out of spouses.

One of the perceived advantages of federation was precisely to restrict entry to the country, and so 'common control over immigration' (Department of Immigration and Multicultural Affairs, 2001) fostered adoption of the Immigration Restriction Act in the same year as federation. From the time of Australian federation, however, Japan progressively assumed a role of greater world significance. This prefigures the wider emergence of Asian power that is a dominant feature of geo-political and economic arrangements today. The early decades of the 20th century saw the rise of militancy in Japan. The Russo-Japanese War of February 1904–September 1905 was fought in Manchuria, on the Yellow Sea and on the Korean peninsula; it ended in a decisive victory for Japan. Japan's success signalled to western powers and to the rest of the world the formidable emergence of a great power, and signalled to colonised peoples that Asian powers were capable of defeating European expansionism. This stoked independence aspirations in several parts of Asia (Jukes, 2002). It was also a major warning to the British state, whose occupation of large parts of Asia was to bring it into direct confrontation with an ever more aggressive Japan. The effects on Japanese Australians and on relations between Australia and Japan, and more indirectly on the Japanese language in Australia, were profound, and included the internment of practically all Australian Japanese during the hostilities of the Pacific War in 1941 (Oliver, 2001). Australia was also. at war with Italy in the early 1940s and in Queensland, South Australia and Western Australia there was also large-scale internment of Italians or 'close watching' of them (Elkner et al., 2005). They were considered enemy aliens if they had not become naturalised, and occasionally even if they had, as in the case of Joe Cantamessa. These circumstances brought together Italians and Japanese in Queensland, animated by what, with the distance of time, seems a bizarre concern that Italian cane-cutters would join up with invading Japanese soldiers in a fifth column to undermine Australian sovereignty.

Australia's Asian relations before the Second World War were partly conducted through colonial agencies, yet even during this time of suspicion and distance from its Asian geographical setting its political leaders, especially Prime Minister Alfred Deakin, spoke of the eventual and inevitable emergence of links with Asia, whether in conflict or in peace (Jayasuriya, 2006).

Australia's loyalties were tied to the British Empire and conflict between Britain and Germany in the second decade of the 20th century involved Australia directly; as a result, at the end of the First World War three Australian states passed legislation banning bilingual education and closing German language schools. Yet it was at this same time that Japanese was introduced into higher education, in 1917 at the University of Sydney and then in 1936 for school students through supplementary programming on Saturdays in Melbourne.

After the conclusion of the Second World War, immigration from Japan remained banned until 1949. Even with the resumption of regular commercial contact and exchange, immigration remained, as it does today, small and often temporary, though the end of the 'white Australia policy' in 1973 saw rapid expansion in exchanges, with the arrival of Japanese businesspeople, tourists, students and marriage partners.

Japanese has a unique role in Australian language education history. In effect, it was the first 'foreign' language Australians collectively decided they needed and wanted to learn (Lo Bianco, 2003, 2009). Japanese was initially part of the broad excluded other, Asia and Asianness, that marked a considerable part of the earliest post-federation policy-making of Australia. There then followed various phases of inclusion of Japanese in public and private education, to its high point, the now inappropriately named 'tsunami' of interest and demand of the late 1980s and early 1990s. As the Japan Foundation has pointed out on several occasions, during this period no country in the world invested more effort in teaching Japanese than Australia and, on a per capital basis, and remarkably for a time in absolute terms as well, more students were enrolled in Japanese foreign language programmes in Australia than in any other country.

The original Australian home for mass Japanese education was Queensland, in the context of the opening up of Australia as a major international tourism destination. During the late 1980s, when mass Japanese tourism to the Great Barrier Reef and the islands and coast of Queensland commenced, Australian labour planners and school career advisers came to recognise a job-related need for language skills. In tourism job advertisements there regularly appeared a requirement for applicants to have a knowledge of Japanese. This link between language competence and advertised jobs, establishing language knowledge as a condition of employment, was a considerable factor in promoting the widespread teaching of Japanese in schools.

The Australian home for Italian education was, by contrast, Melbourne and later Adelaide, mainly in areas of industrial or rural industrial employment. So here we see two significantly different sociological realities in evidence. The Italian one is premised on the second-generation effects of mass industrial migration, though of course it builds on earlier Australian visits to and encounters with elite Italian culture, as noted by Moss (see above), but in the context of a longer history of cultural exchange as well as individual adventurism and exploration (Kent *et al.*, 2010). Australian encounters with Japan and its national culture came later were mediated first by individual contact, then by political and strategic relations; there followed hostility and conflict, reconciliation and trade, commercial interdependence and then mass two-way tourism and cultural learning.

Post-war migration

Italy and Japan share the experience of 20th-century nationalist militarism and indeed were allied in the Axis powers during the Second World War, whose belligerence culminated in defeat, although in the final years of the war the Italian state was formally an ally of Australia. In both cases new regimes were established after the cessation of hostilities: Japan emerged as a constitutional monarchy enshrined in its constitution of 3 May 1947 and Italy formed itself into a constitutional republic via referendum on 2 June 1946.

After the internment as enemy aliens of Australians of Italian and Japanese origin (many of whom had been resident in Australia for long periods and naturalised, while others were Australian born and legal citizens), rehabilitation proceeded. The war had provoked a sense of economic and strategic vulnerability in Australia, hence the commencement of the post-war migration programme, recruiting new settlers, mainly initially from Britain. Under Labour Prime Minister Ben Chifley, Australia determined that it needed a 1% annual population increase, established a Department of Immigration and launched it under the leadership of its first Minister for Immigration, Arthur Calwell, with the slogan 'populate or perish' (Price, 1998; Price & Hugo, 2000). The twin goals of bolstering defence and fostering development were at the forefront of the plan, hence the preference for permanent settlers. In addition to the admission of displaced persons and refugees from eastern Europe, the bulk of the immigration intake consisted of free and permanent settlers, as 'new Australians'. The aim of a 1% annual population increase was sustained until the Whitlam government of the early 1970s and has fluctuated since. Migration has contributed some 7 million people to the overall population since 1945, out of a current total population of 22 million.

The Immigration Restriction Act of 1901, and its general spirit, influenced administration of the post-war migration programme, hence the strong preference for British immigrants, with an initial target that '9 out of 10' would be British, modified to include southern Europeans when the proportion of British was no longer sustainable, despite their receiving considerable incentives to relocate to Australia. The reduction in British entrants provoked alarm and led to restrictions on the numbers of southern Europeans (Jupp, 2007) and a compensatory programme of 'Bring out a Briton' adopted in the mid to late 1950s. Over time, renewed prosperity in Europe made attracting new immigrants from there more difficult and gradual improvement in attitudes towards other nationalities led to the relenting of pro-British immigration policies, culminating in the adoption by the Whitlam government in 1972 of a non-discrimination principle in immigrant recruitment. This signified the formal end of the white Australia policy. From the commencement of the migration programme in 1949, Italian arrivals constituted the second largest number in each decade to 1970 (Department of Immigration and Multicultural Affairs, 2001), and third largest in the decade between 1971 and 1980, but dropped sharply thereafter.

A crucial point in Australian commercial relations with both Italy and Japan was the admission of the United Kingdom to the then European Economic Community (EEC) in 1973. This deprived Australian exporters of direct access to the UK market, and from the late 1970s the already established Australian commercial relationship with Japan expanded quickly, until Japan became Australia's premier export partner. From the UK's accession to the EEC both Asian regionalism and domestic Australian multiculturalism begin to shape foreign policy and economics directly, and came to have a direct impact on cultural policy and language education choices.

While commercial relations between Italy and Australia are smaller than those between Japan and Australia, they remain substantial and the trade relationship is complementary, with Australian imports and exports broadly aligned across the main categories of production. Tourism from Japan to Australia has weakened and migration and intermarriage have expanded. The effects of these changes have been to diversify and expand the bases of the national relationships with Australia.

Japanese remained exotic, and strictly foreign and distant in its earliest presence in Australian education, and then assumed strategic and geo-political interest from the mid-1930s, growing slowly in the era of domination of Australian political life by Robert Menzies as Prime Minister, when the first commercial links were made and the germs of an Asian consciousness emerged in the wake of Australian trade connections to the region.

Language Policy on Italian and Japanese

Through the 1970s and much of the 1980s, the Italian and Japanese languages remained on parallel tracks in Australia, with essentially different purposes in education and directed at different audiences. In the mid-1980s, however, they were brought together as 'key languages' for Australia, a category created in the National Policy on Languages of 1987, adopted by the Hawke government, Australia's first formal language policy, only then to diverge dramatically in the heyday of 'Asia literacy', with the prioritisation of funding exclusively for Asian languages in the 1994 National Asian Languages and Studies in Australian Schools strategy (NALSAS, 1994–2002). Today, both Italian and Japanese are normalised presences in public education, but the Italian language struggles to retain its prominence against the greater interest in, promotion of and funding for Asian languages and the ageing of the Italo-Australian community. Japanese is also beset by problems, such as the greater interest that has been directed towards China and Chinese, and the effects of too rapid an expansion from the late 1980s. For both languages there is the enervating problem of public expectation, since many programmes lacked rigour and their failure to deliver learning proficiency was a problem.

Many labels have been attached to the two languages in Australian edu cation: the most enduring ones have been 'trade' and 'community' language, sometimes European and Asian. The two languages are like 'condensed symbols', carrying a range of implicit meanings about society, its choices, direction and self-image. They entered the school system for very different reasons, responding to markedly different policy agendas. As a result, Italian and Japanese exemplify the two 'vintages' of policy ambition we have been discussing: multiculturalism and Asia literacy. Each has been championed at different times, by different interests and with different rationales. The multicultural and the Asianist discourses have made emblematic claims for a new kind of Australia in the making. We can see, even at the textual level, how each has shaped the words and paragraphs of policy and the press releases of ministers, the legitimations of school principals, letters to parents and opinion pieces in the newspapers.

However, the positions Italian and Japanese hold and the reasons they are taught are complicated by other languages claiming space, for overlapping and different purposes, and responding to other interests. Both are vulnerable to 'other' Asian and 'other' European languages, and, because neither Italian nor Japanese is a large world language (instead they are national languages of developed single economies with considerable international spread through diasporas), they are vulnerable to claims made by 'bigger' languages, spoken in more nations and present in a greater number of international institu-tions. For Japanese this challenging other appears to be Chinese; for Italian, it appears to be Spanish. In Australian education, Japanese has coexisted with Indonesian, and Italian with French and German, for long periods of time, each producing a conceptual map of 'regions of the world' (Asia; Europe), historical projections (the past; the future), cultural orientations (east; west) and legitimations (economy; tradition).

The Italian and Japanese Diasporas

The devastation of the Second World War plunged both Italy and Japan into poverty. In the Italian case this was alleviated only through mass migration, where the scale of emigration to Australia was second only to that in the late 19th century to the Americas, north and south. Japan also had experience of mass migration in the 19th century, with the largest outflow to Brazil, followed by the United States, Canada and Peru (Maidment & Mackerras, 1998). In the post-war Japanese diaspora, known as *Nikkei*, emigrants and their descendants account for some 2.5 million people. Japanese has become a clearly established language of 'heritage' in the United States, a characteristic and a perception it mostly lacks in Australia, though many small and active Japanese language community schools are well established. Today, some 5 million Brazilians and 1.2 million Americans count direct Japanese ancestry, by far the two largest components of the *Nikkei* (Masterson & Funada-Classen, 2004), with numbers exceeding 100,000 in the Philippines, and between 50,000 and 100,000 in Peru and Canada. The Australian total is more modest, at approximately 20,000.

In Japan in the 1980s, labour recruitment policies for industrial jobs led many ethnic Japanese migrants (and their offspring) to return to the country. While cities such as Nagoya now are home to significant numbers of Spanish- and Portuguese-speaking Japanese-origin immigrants (Tsuda, 2003), often the bonds of ethnicity do not overcome their feeling of being 'strangers', in a complex interplay of identities. The term 'return migration' implies that, for example, Brazilians of Japanese descent moving as unskilled foreign workers to Japanese cities are 'going home'. The second largest group of 'foreigners' in Japan are the estimated 280,000 Brazilian Japanese (Tsuda, 2003), but they identify culturally as Brazilian. Moreover, because the language shift to Portuguese had been well established by the third generation (Hiroki & Loveday, 1998), these returnees encounter the Japanese language as essentially a distant second or foreign language of heritage. This means that the great bulk of Japanese teaching in the world is essentially foreign language education, and to foster this the Japanese government in 1972 established the Japan Foundation. This is the nation's official cultural body, operating under the Ministry of Foreign Affairs; it offers testing services, cultural exchange and teaching, among many other activities as stated on its website:

> The Japan Foundation responds extensively to overseas demands for Japanese-language education in ways such as dispatching specialists to overseas Japanese educational organizations and training local Japanese-language teachers. (http://www.jpf.go.jp/e)

In contrast, the Italian diaspora is larger, older and more widespread, representing some 25 million people, whose numbers are best estimated in terms of ancestry rather than birthplace, given its historic origins. Like the *Nikkei*, the *oriundi* have very large representation in South America, but are very strongly represented in northern Europe, some parts of Africa, Australia and North America (Totaro-Genevois, 2005). The great size and dispersion of the Italian diaspora has meant that language maintenance activities abroad are more diffuse, with elements of top-down and bottom-up activity, as they draw on support from local community groups, regional governments and associations, which negotiate with Italian government official groups. The Italian law from which subsidies to programmes offering Italian teaching abroad is authorised was designed for the temporary migra tion outflows to Belgium and Germany from the 1950s and 1960s, while the bulk of its enrolled students in Toronto, Buenos Aires and Melbourne are locally born citizens. Local arrangements for language maintenance usually complement but sometimes tangle with official representations of the culture in schooling and the official organs of the state which support Italian as a 'foreign' language abroad. The worldwide network of Italian cultural institutes (http://www.sfiic.org) represents what might be called state-authorised culture promotion abroad, under the Ministry of Foreign Affairs. The locally based and constituted Dante Alighieri Societies, among dozens of other agencies based on locality or region, make local efforts to transmit and support the Italian language and culture.

Italian mass migration (Church, 2005) began in a similar period to Japan's and coincided with the political and monarchical unification of Italy in 1861. It lasted almost exactly a century, disrupted only during the 20 years of Fascist rule, when the outflow of population was directed to the settlement of Italy's colonies in Libya and the Horn of Africa. It accelerated rapidly after the Second World War and only definitively ceased with Italy's 'economic miracle' of the 1960s and 1970s, when the country was transformed from a peasant agrarian economy to an urban industrialised one, then the world's sixth largest, able to offer employment to its people. The high point of departure was between 1900 and 1913, immediately preceding the First World War. In this period such large numbers left that the permanent net outflow was 25 million, constituting one of the largest net movements of people in modern history.

As a result, some 25 million Brazilians (around 15% of the national population), 20 million Argentines (50%), 18 million Americans (6%), 1.5 million Canadians (4.5%), 5 million French (9%), 1 million Uruguayans (29%) and 916,100 Australians (4.6% of the population) count recent Italian heritage, with significant numbers in Venezuela, Peru and Belgium (Favero & Tassello, 1978; Sori, 1979).

Like Japan, Italy has a long history of emigration followed by a short history of immigration, initially of *Nikkei* and *oriundi*, respectively, and now strongly of people from all parts of the world. As a result, both languages, essentially national rather than global in character, have very active 'second language immigrant' and 'second language emigrant' sociologies that are influencing how they are spoken and used in their home countries and abroad.

Victoria

In Chapter 1 we located our research in the context of the vigorous and volatile national language policy scene. In this context the prominent voices are typically top down in direction, voices which claim to represent the 'national interest'. Education in Australia, however, rests with state governments and is delivered by 'jurisdictions' of government, as well as by independent and Catholic schools. The federal government is able to gain traction over education by several means, mostly indirect. It can tie funding to new policy initiatives, administer national tests and engage in comparative research of outcomes across states and systems; it can also exercise influence through the coordination of national effort. Via these mechanisms the federal government has managed to influence curriculum development and other education policy, although education delivery and overall responsibility for education remains the constitutional preserve of states and territories. In some areas, notably Indigenous and immigrant education, federal responsibility is more direct. Through immigrant recruitment policies and the delivery of settlement services to new arrivals, the federal government has shaped immigrant language education directly.

Language policy has been an area of extensive cooperation between state and federal levels of government, with many federal initiatives beginning as state policies. Victoria has a reputation for having the most extensive and best-supported language policy in Australia; it enjoys the widest range of languages taught and retains the highest percentage of year 12 students in languages (Lo Bianco & Slaughter, 2009). Victorian policy for languages has mirrored federal initiatives and influenced them in turn. In the period of research covered by this volume, Victorian language education policy was a subject of experimentation and debate, influenced by two main documents: *Languages for Victoria's Future* (Victorian Department of Education and Training, 2002) and the state-wide common curriculum framework, the *Victorian Essential Learning Standards* (Victorian Curriculum and Assessment Authority, 2007). Unlike in the federal sphere, where multicultural policy was downplayed by the Howard government in favour of assimilation and downplayed also by the Rudd and Gillard governments, which preferred to advance Asian trade foreign languages, multicultural policy has remained well supported in Victoria. In 2009 the state's Labour government issued a document entitled *Education for Global and Multicultural Citizenship*, a strategy intended to cover 2009–13. In the Foreword, the Minister for Education stated:

> Victoria is a thriving multicultural society. Our population hails from over 230 nations, speaks 180 languages and dialects and follows more than 116 religions. Advances in communications and transport technology, increasing global migration and new forms of cultural exchange have led to the rapid globalisation of our society and economy. In the 21st century, at school, in work and in life, we are interacting across cultures. Now and into the future, therefore, we must prepare our students for global and multicultural citizenship ... knowledge, skills and attitudes required for active global and multicultural citizenship.... More than ever before, intercultural skills, high-level English skills, proficiency in at least one language other than English and information communication technology skills are of critical importance for our students. Knowledge of multicultural perspectives and of emerging global issues, and an open, respectful, compassionate attitude to difference are also vital.... Students who possess the skills, knowledge and attitudes of a global and multicultural citizen will have a competitive edge and contribute to our national advantage. (Bronwyn Pike MP, in State of Victoria, 2009)

The tone and content of this declaration are consonant with the first of the federal policy statements discussed in Chapter 1, the National Statement and Plan, in its inclusive scope and wide remit. However, just as the three federal policies are hierarchically organised, with some having the force and backing of funding, explicit targets and pressure, while others attract less support and have to rely on persuasion, argument and local interest to gain traction in schools, exactly the same dynamic occurs in the official texts of state policy. This means that all-embracing declarations like *Education for Global and Multicultural Citizenship* typically are converted into concrete action at school and district level only when there is local interest in doing so.

In late 2010, shortly after the Victorian Labour government commenced a process of public consultation to devise a new state language education policy, it was defeated in a state election. The incoming Liberal–National government declared a strong commitment to a new and ambitious programme of support for languages, aiming to consolidate Victoria's place as the national leader in language education.

During the course of our school-based research, the state language education policy was expressed in the 2002 report *Languages for Victoria's Future*. This policy affirmed the 'importance of languages in the core curriculum for all Victorian students and the expectations that all students in Years

P–10 learn a language' (p. vii). It also recommended that schools 'provide opportunities for all students in Early, Middle & Later Years to learn another language' (p. vii). Additionally, it created 'three Centres of Excellence ... to take the lead in the innovative use of ICT, online and multimedia materials and act as lighthouse schools that promote ICT for languages and skill teachers in its use' (p. ix). It was through one of these Centres of Excellence that our research was conducted.

The design of the curriculum is contained in the 2005 *Victorian Essential Learning Standards*, adopted by the Victorian Curriculum and Assessment Authority (VCAA) to 'provide a new approach to organising the curriculum in schools' (VCAA, 2007: 1). The standards provide a planning framework for the school curriculum that integrates three interrelated strands of activity in education: physical, personal and social learning; discipline-based learning; and interdisciplinary learning. Each of these strands contains a learning domain, which most people would know as a 'school subject', which the VCCA calls 'a description of essential knowledge, skills and behaviours within a Strand'. Among these, under the strand of discipline-based learning, there is a learning domain called 'English and language'. Each of these domains is further divided into 'dimensions'. For the language domain the two dimensions are: communicating in language; and intercultural knowledge and language awareness.

This is the curriculum design framework for the languages taught in the schools in which our research took place. For each dimension there is a set of 'standards' which 'describe what students should know and how well, and identify what is important for students to achieve at different stages of their schooling, and provide a clear basis for reporting and planning' (VCAA, 2007: 1). Finally, there are two pathways for learners to pursue the domain through its dimensions, described as follows in the *Victorian Essential Learning Standards* document: pathway 1 is for students who begin learning a language in primary school and continue to study the same language to year 10; and pathway 2 is for students who begin learning a language only at secondary school, in year 7 (Victorian Curriculum and Assessment Authority, 2007).

A particular complication with the design of the languages curriculum is that the standards are delayed, introduced for assessment and reporting only from level 4 (see below), rather than from the commencement of schooling. The justification for postponing the assessment of language in the earliest phase of learning is as follows:

> While it is clear that students gain most benefit from the study of another language when they begin this study in the early years, it is

acknowledged that some schools choose to maximise the effect of their resources by introducing language programs at different year levels with appropriate time allocations. In recognition of the cumulative nature of language learning, the language domain includes progression measures, which provide a typical sequence of second language development leading to Level 4. Regardless of the level at which the study of a language other than English is introduced, students will need to develop the knowledge and skills described in the progression measures before they attempt the learning associated with the Level 4 standards. These progression measures also assist those schools that provide language programs prior to Years 5 and 6 to assess and report effectively on student achievement. (Victorian Curriculum and Assessment Authority, 2007: 7)

The language policy documents at the federal level discussed in Chapter 1 show an increasing focus on economic strategies and progress-ively less emphasis on multiculturalism. This move away from community concerns for language selection was somewhat attenuated at state level, especially in Victoria, which has seen its constituencies for community/heritage language provision remain strong. The idea of 'key' or priority languages which has percolated from federal government has, however, shaped local choices and influenced some aspects of state policy, but the state's commitment to a wide range of languages and rich diversity in provision has remained unchanged for 20 years. Thus, the background of the research into the learning Italian and Japanese in schools reported in the present volume has two facets: a broad context of official texts at the federal level, with their declarations of policy intention focusing strongly on Asian regionalism and trade, set against debates and argument about the interpretation and priorities of those official documents; and the specific Victorian context, in which this documentation and debate percolates into the learning of Italian and Japanese in schools.

3 The Research Approach and the Schools

The data-gathering for our study was done between 2005 and 2011 in the western suburbs of Melbourne, the capital of Victoria, within the Victorian Education Department's 'western metropolitan' zone. The setting and aims of the study and the methods of data collection used in the research – Q-methodology, focus groups, surveys and language journals – are described in this chapter. In addition, demographic survey data are presented for the study area, drawn from a range of sources – administrators, teachers, parents and students – together with an overview of students' language use in the school, home and broader community. The Q-methodology data are provided in Chapter 4.

The Setting

The term 'western suburbs' designates an area of the metropolis of Melbourne that comprises several municipalities and a variety of socio-economic conditions. The area has several large heavy-industrial zones. The area is socio-economically mixed, but predominantly working class to lower middle class, and has a long history of immigrant settlement. There are pockets of gentrification, and these are characterised by an increase in service-based economic enterprises and institutions of higher education, as well as some pockets of expensive middle-class housing, with 'boutique' enclaves of heritage architecture where growing numbers of relatively prosperous professionals reside. The area is bounded on three sides by the semi-rural and rural outskirts of the city, the southern edge of Port Phillip Bay and the Port of Melbourne, and the inner-city suburbs. In the precincts of the schools involved in the study, the suburbs would be best described as of low socio-economic status, with a fading industrial post-war employ-ment base.

Many residents are the descendants of the first large wave of immigration to Australia, from the post-war migration scheme discussed in Chapter 2, the generation that introduced to the Australian demographic make-up its very high proportion of Mediterranean immigrants, principally from Italy, Greece, the former Yugoslavia, Turkey, Lebanon and Malta. There were two later 'waves' of new arrivals to the western suburbs: Indochinese refugees in the 1970s and 1980s, when Cambodian, Laotian and Vietnamese immigrants settled in large numbers; and more recently asylum-seekers from a large variety of countries, mainly from the Horn of Africa and South and Central Asia. These three broad groupings of immigrants – those from the Mediterranean, Indochina, and Africa or Central and South Asia – are differentiated by their immigration status (respectively, in general terms, recruited mass labourers, refugees, asylum-seekers, but also recruited skilled workers, displaced persons, humanitarian entrants, and those seeking family reunions) and their subsequent socio-economic fortunes.

There were four schools involved in the study, for which we use pseudonyms: two primary schools, Kangaroo Paw Primary and Wattle Tree Primary; and two secondary schools, Billabong High and River Gum High. The two secondary schools teach both Italian and Japanese, while the two primary schools teach only one each: Italian at Wattle Tree and Japanese at Kangaroo Paw. In the primary schools, only students in years 5 and 6 participated in the research, while in the secondary schools students from all year levels were involved.

Kangaroo Paw Primary is the longest-established school; its main building dates from the late 1880s. It is located in an inner north-western suburb, a long-settled quiet residential area. Although the majority of the school's 500 enrolments are from the immediate vicinity, an increasing number of students come from surrounding areas. A large proportion of students are from relatively affluent families and a little more than a quarter are from a home where English is a second language. At Kangaroo Paw Primary, Japanese is taught by two teachers (one a Japanese native speaker); students in years 2–6 learn the language for two hours a week. Japanese is integrated in the topics that the class undertakes each term. Extensive use is made of information and communication technology (ICT) and authentic materials are used to develop understandings of and familiarity with Japan.

Wattle Tree Primary opened in the early 1990s and is in an outer north-western suburb. It is a medium-size school (700 enrolments); a high proportion of the school population is in the low socio-economic bracket. With over 40 languages represented in the school population, more than 70% of the students have English as a second language. Ten classes of students in years 5 and 6 participate in two one-hour sessions of Italian each week. The Italian topics are linked to the integrated themes presented in the classroom. The teacher, who is of Italian background, also provides a cultural and linguistic awareness programme for two sessions each term to the 10 classes of students in years 3 and 4.

Billabong High School, established in the mid-1950s, is a single-campus secondary college located in an inner north-western suburb, a residential area only a few kilometres from the city centre. The school's catchment area is comparatively socio-economically secure, and so only a small proportion of students are in receipt of education subsidies; relatively few students are from homes where English is not the main language. Students in year 7 study either Japanese or Italian for three 55-minute sessions each week and continue it until the end of year 8. Languages become elective in year 9 and in the post-compulsory years students' activities become more focused on gaining a deeper understanding of life in the target countries, as well as on achieving higher proficiency in the language. Students have an opportunity to go on school trips to Italy or Japan, and students taking Japanese can interact with students from a Japanese sister school, who regularly visit Billabong High School.

The fourth school in the study, River Gum High, was established in the early 1990s and comprises two junior campuses for students in years 7–10 and one senior campus for students in years 11 and 12 (it was one of the first multi-campus schools in the north-west area of Melbourne). River Gum High has a total enrolment of 1800 students; the proportion of students receiving education support reflects the overall socio-economic make-up of western Melbourne; however, a relatively low proportion speak a second language at home. The school has a commitment to provide all students with the opportunity to study either Italian or Japanese in years 7–10 and has strong exchange programmes with schools in both countries. Students at River Gum High participate in three 55-minute sessions each week and the school is committed to the ongoing development of engaging languages programmes that are responsive to the needs of students.

Aims of the Research

Our study aimed to ascertain how and why the ambitious policies on language education in Australia, set out in Chapter 1, had met such uneven success and to document and describe the concrete reality of language education in ordinary schools and among ordinary learners. A second aim was to document the sociologies of Italian and Japanese, whose presence in schooling in Australia, as described in Chapter 2, epitomises two distinct phases of recent national language planning, multiculturalism and Asia literacy. A third overarching aim was to document experience, that is, how language learning plans, conceived in far-away cabinet meeting rooms, conference halls and academic settings actually 'play out' when they arrive in schools. How do learners actually experience these plans for them and their lingual futures? What do they really feel, as much as think, about the experiences they are obliged or encouraged to have in schools on behalf of abstract ideas of national reconstruction? Importantly, we also investigated how the reactions of the students can be seen as a component of the overall activity of 'language planning policy'.

We were also keen to explore new and innovative research methodologies. These new methods were selected to document 'subjectivity', that is, the lived and personal accounts of learners, as unobtrusively as possible. The idea of listening to the learner is often proclaimed in research studies of second language acquisition, but learner experience is far less commonly studied in research on language policy. Instead, language planning studies tend to relegate learners to numerical representation of outcomes from funding allocations and learners become merely vehicles for achieving the goals of language policy-makers. Typically, the numbers of enrolled students are noted and their performance tracked, mostly through examination results, or attrition and persistence rates.

Research Methodology

Diachronic research

This component of the research investigated the perspectives of various groups of stakeholders over the five-year duration of the research (2005–11), to identify perceptions of the teaching of languages and to determine opportunities for the enhancement of the Italian and Japanese programmes. The diachronic focus allowed us to observe whether reactions to the aims of language policy altered over time.

The tools used in the diachronic research included a range of surveys. The language coordinators and teachers in the four participating schools were directly involved in the gathering and discussion of data, and as co-researchers as well as respondents they assisted in the formulation of ideas about how the implementation of the language education policies in the schools was an active policy-making process in itself, rather than passive implementation of outsiders' plans. These teacher participants were supplied with a research book, which contained information about the purpose and the components of the study as well as instructions and materials for the completion of the surveys. They administered the surveys to their students and made the research instruments and documentation available to parents and staff in their schools. They even assisted in the design of some of the instruments.

Five surveys of the school community were undertaken:

(1) A survey of administrators aimed to collect information about management and planning issues, such as staffing, timetabling, curriculum support and external funding.
(2) A survey of staff (teachers in disciplines other than languages) gathered information about the links between language teaching and other domains of study, as well as the attitudes and beliefs of staff from other disciplines towards languages. It also sought ideas about possible areas of collaboration between teachers from other disciplines or classes and language teachers.
(3) A survey of language teachers was designed to gather data about the specific challenges they faced in the teaching of Italian or Japanese.
(4) A survey of parents collected information about their attitudes to and perceptions of Italian or Japanese, as well as other languages.
(5) A student survey covered their language background and previous study, their perceptions of their language ability and the usefulness of languages, their attitudes to other cultures and societies, their response to the Italian or Japanese curriculum, and their intentions regarding future language studies. One survey instrument was tailored for primary students and another for students at secondary school.

Students also completed language journals to provide a running record, over specified periods, of their use of languages at school, at home and in the community (which language had been used, with whom, where and why).

The analysis of the survey data is discussed later in this chapter.

Synchronic (intensive) research: Focus groups and Q-methodology

Although statistics derived from the continuing survey research enabled us to gain a comprehensive picture of perceptions of and attitudes to languages, an intensive research component concentrating specifically on secondary students was used to deepen and extend this information. The students involved in the intensive research comprised those deemed by their teachers to be very committed to languages and similar numbers of students deemed to be uncertain about or uninterested in continuing with languages after the compulsory years. The methods used were focus group interviews and Q-methodology.

In focus group interviews students were asked about the Italian and Japanese programmes at their school, their feelings about languages, how languages related to their future as well as their interest in and intentions for future study. In addition to providing information about this particular cohort of students and in-depth comments on issues students thought important, the focus group interviews were used to identify two sets of 25 key statements that were later used in a Q-sort.

Q-methodology was used to collect, analyse and interpret data to show students' deep beliefs about the teaching and learning of Italian and Japanese. The 25 statements students were asked to sort using a predetermined distribution pattern were mostly opinions rather than facts, though some factual statements were included, and for the most part were the comments gathered during the focus group interviews. We called this the 'concourse' of statements about each topic, that is, what the students' peers typically say about the subjects, and this formed the Q-sample. These statements were ranked by the participants according to their personal point of view. The concourse covered six areas: teaching, learning the language, the 'relevance' of the curriculum, the value of learning the language, classroom control and organisational aspects of language provision. Some of the same students who took part in the focus group interviews also participated in the Q-study, giving additional validity to the final results.

Analysis of the data gathered as part of the intensive research is reported in Chapter 4.

Overview of the Study

In the first year of the study (2005), administrators, teachers and parents were asked to complete surveys so that their perspectives on the teaching of languages could be determined, in part to identify ways in which the Italian and Japanese programmes in the four schools could be enhanced.

Students were asked to complete surveys and two language journals, both in the first year of the study and again in the second year of the school-based component of the research. While there were many commonalities in the design of the research instruments, some of the areas in the surveys were specifically tailored to primary students and others were relevant to secondary students.

Once analysed, the extensive set of data provided deep and triangulated information on key issues.

While a range of quantitative and qualitative measures are available for exploring the experience and outcomes of teaching languages, to inform policy and implementation, we selected Q-methodology (Brown, 1980;

Stephenson, 1953) because of its unique mix of techniques to gather both quantitative and qualitative data, to systematically investigate students' beliefs and attitudes. The description of Q and its application, as well as the results of the Q research, appear in Chapter 4. The students and the schools that provided the data are typical of students and large urban schools in similar areas across Australia. The general aspiration of the study is to inform future policy development with evidence of language learning as it proceeds in the circumstances typical of public education.

Although it is possible to incorporate into Q-methodology itself attitudinal measures such as surveys, questionnaires and interviews, it is used here because it also offers a way of exploring themes and issues drawn from other data-gathering instruments. Here, statements made by students about the experience of language study, and their responses to what policy-makers expect of them, were presented back to the students for ranking. In this way we had an extended and deep engagement with how learners experience and feel about language study. They were required to weight their own opinions against those of their peers as well as to discuss these both directly with the researchers and in focus groups.

This wide-ranging approach permits a more robust investigation of attitudes than is available with other methods, especially those that require the researcher to offer respondents a series of researcher-devised options for response. Instead, Q-methods allowed us to gather important insights into the factors that shaped the students' stance with respect to language learning and the preservation of their home language, for example.

In the commentary that follows italics denote remarks made by the survey respondents and the figures in parentheses are percentages of the total number of respondents completing the relevant survey items.

Language teachers, a key element

The critical importance of having highly qualified and competent language teachers was consistently evidenced. Having appropriately *trained teachers* was considered by administrators (67%), teachers from other disciplines (65%), language teachers (62%) and parents (27%) to be of paramount importance for a *successful language programme*. The *lack of experienced and competent teachers* was a specific concern expressed by the language teachers themselves, especially in relation to any lengthy period of teaching cover.

Administrators (50%) and languages staff (39%) considered the availability of *professional language teachers* to be a key factor in whether Italian or Japanese was among the *subjects offered* at the school. When it came to the *uptake of language*, administrators (50%), languages teachers (23%) and teachers from other disciplines (20%) agreed that the calibre of the language teacher was an important factor in whether students included languages in their choice of subjects.

The quality of the teacher as well as *the commitment and quality of the teaching staff* and the fact that language programmes had *great teachers* who were *qualified and enthusiastic* were seen by all administrators as the strengths of the programmes in their schools. Parents suggested that *enthusiasm was needed to make the children strive to learn to read, write and speak their language* and considered the success of the programme and in some instances the fact that their children were continuing with their languages study were *due in no small way to the teacher's enthusiasm and teaching methods.*

In summary, both staff and parents saw language teachers as the crucial element of any language programme and believed that their availability determined the existence of the programme and that their expertise, commitment and enthusiasm were paramount for the longevity of the programme and students success in language learning.

Languages in the school curriculum

When talking about the place of languages in the school curriculum, staff commented on: (1) how they could support the Italian and Japanese programmes in their schools, (2) what they considered to be good language pedagogies, and (3) ways in which they could collaborate across disciplines. Briefly, supportive attitudes were seen as a clear expression of the value placed on learning languages but practical activities could also be carried out to demonstrate support. Pedagogy, curriculum materials and teachers who made language learning relevant and meaningful for students were deemed to be important, and staff were able to identify many ways in which languages could be integrated in the school curriculum, as the more detailed comments below demonstrate.

Supporting languages

Language teachers commented on the importance of supportive attitudes and the fact that *schools, local community and parents needed to make a clear show of support for language* and value it as a subject. Although general promotion of the programme was mentioned by both administrators and teachers from other disciplines (40%), the latter also proposed they could *support* the Italian or Japanese programme in their schools by *taking an interest* and *supporting language as a subject choice for students by encouraging them to take it* and also by highlighting *the link between learning a language other than English and gaining a stronger understanding of English*. Staff believed they could further support languages in very practical ways related to the curriculum (36%) or to specific activities (30%), and could offer practical assistance by sharing either some of their expertise or the facilities at their disposal, or by actively using the language. Administrators, on the other hand, thought they could *support* language teaching not only by being encouraging of both the programme as a whole and specific activities but also by making *timetabling decisions to maintain classes* and to *provide adequate time* for lessons, and they acknowledged that an insufficient time allowance would seriously compromise programme quality.

Good teaching practice

Language teachers and teachers from other disciplines both placed importance on pedagogy and materials, but for the former the main factor (46%) that contributed to *good language teaching practice* was the teachers themselves. They believed language teachers need to enjoy what they teach and to be dedicated and skilled, and require *enthusiasm and a passion for teaching language.* Ultimately, a language teacher who *knows his/her content and who can deliver it even in a 'challenging' environment* was seen as a key factor in effective language teaching. Teachers from other disciplines identified activities (54%) as the crucial factor. They believed *good language education* needs to involve a *variety of activities to reinforce language* and to provide *hands-on, engaging activities that are linked to real-life situations.* These teachers believed that making languages meaningful for students, including *lots of immersion activities so that the language is used constantly in different situations and in real contexts,* incorporating in the language programme excursions, study tours, guest speakers or activities that promote deeper cultural understanding would ensure learning was *related to students' lives and experiences* and therefore would constitute sound pedagogical practice.

Languages across the curriculum

Teachers from other disciplines identified many ways in which they could or did in fact collaborate with their languages colleagues and these included both broad curriculum areas (59%) and specific activities (38%). For the former, teachers' suggestions included *planning integrated units* and an *integrated curriculum across faculties.* Some examples were given for specific subjects: *History where the examination of ancient or medieval Japan and Rome currently occurred but links were not explicit; English, where students could read Japanese or Italian histories and use a range of sources and texts that originated from these cultures;* home economics *include more of these cuisines;* and *allowing students to integrate parts of geography with Japan or Italy.* The use of technology, film-making, audio-recording and editing were also mentioned as possible areas of collaboration within the curriculum. The comments made about specific activities suggested collaboration could be achieved by *supporting 'activities' run by the language faculty* – such as providing *assistance with Language Week, assisting with excursions, participating in cultural activities, attending functions, having students perform at language functions* or being involved in *food preparation activities* and also by *assisting with work requirements in SOSE-related issues* (SOSE is Studies of Society and Environment).

Languages in the community

When looking at languages in the community, the comments included in the parents' surveys were the main source of evidence. While 60% of parents who returned a survey spoke only English at home, nearly half of all parents overall believed that it was very important for their children to *learn a language* (48%) and a large minority (32%) thought it was very important specifically to *learn Italian or Japanese* at school.

The vast majority of parents thought their children enjoyed languages (78%) and they reported having *high expectations* regarding their children's fluency and proficiency in the language (27%), enjoyment of the subject (14%) and attainment of cultural (12%) as well as linguistic awareness (10%), as the comments below illustrate.

Parents hoped that the language programme would enable their children to *converse adequately in the community* so that they would *become fluent and confident* and not only be able *to converse confidently in the language with a native speaker* and *learn enough to be able to use it in society* but also be able *to proficiently speak, read and write* the language. Parents further hoped their children *would enjoy learning another language*. Some wanted their children *to keep enjoying the programme*, while others wished their children *would begin to enjoy it more*. Culturally, parents expected the programme to *encourage acceptance and interest in other cultures* and enable their children to *begin to understand more of another culture, another way of doing things* and to *become familiar with important aspects*, because if the children *learn about … culture, understand and accept the differences* this would *enable them to appreciate another culture and to respect it*. Parents also mentioned their expectation that the language programme would give their children *a good understanding of other languages* so that they could *have a more thorough understanding of grammar, pronunciation, vocabulary* and also *fully understand the nature of the language*.

Although parents believed the language teacher was the key person when their children needed assistance with either Italian or Japanese, they agreed to varying degrees that they had a *role* in their children's learning of languages. They generally felt that the school provided *information* about what their children learned, how they were taught and how they progressed in Italian and Japanese. Ultimately what parents seemed to be looking for was *the instillation of a 'want' to learn the language* and that their children *should enjoy the whole experience* because *if the child enjoys it, then it is a good thing.*

Languages and student motivation

Language teachers and teachers from other disciplines appear divided in their views of student motivation to learn a language. The percentage of language teachers who believed students had low motivation was higher (62%) than the percentage who felt this was not the case (30%), while half of the teachers from other disciplines were not sure about this. Other comments about student motivation were similarly divided between affirmative and negative responses. It was suggested that *students seemed to be very interested or totally uninterested in studying languages* and ultimately *the students who experienced success were very motivated to showcase their abilities while others with less success ... dropped it like a hot potato.*

Recurring themes concerned attitudes, content and methodology. Four issues affecting motivation were identified: (1) the difficulty or rigour of the subject, (2) the value accorded to the subject, (3) the compulsory nature of the subject, and (4) teaching methods and curriculum. The first two issues were mentioned by both language teachers and teachers from other disciplines, while the third and fourth issues were raised only by language teachers.

Difficulty or rigour

Language teachers remarked on the difficulty of the subject (54%) and claimed that languages were *perceived as being 'difficult' and a lot of work*, suggesting that *students considered language a hard option and often chose subjects considered to be easier.* Similarly, teachers from other disciplines (19%) believed that if students *found language acquisition difficult they would not want to continue.* They further suggested students *may drop Italian/Japanese because the work is more structured and discipline oriented which students may find too challenging* and the level of *abstraction required to learn a second language i.e. empathy, the ability to imagine its usefulness, was difficult for adolescents in the same way as maths.*

Value

Positive attitudes to languages were considered important. Language teachers commented on the value accorded to language as a subject (31%) and suggested students lacked motivation because they did *not feel the importance of learning languages.* This was corroborated by teachers from other disciplines, who gave as their second main reason for the lack of motivation the fact that languages were generally not valued (11%) and *most students couldn't see the value of learning a different language or how it could be useful to them in the future.* Furthermore, these teachers suggested that it was not only students who placed little value on the learning of another language but also parents, who *didn't see the relevance of the subject, there was a general community* habit *to consider language in schools as being secondary to other subjects,* and, likewise, many teachers did not support the programme.

Compulsory nature

A number of language teachers (23%) believed that making languages compulsory further reduced student motivation, although one teacher suggested that it was *difficult to compare with other subjects because some subjects were still compulsory in the VCE* [Victorian Certificate of Education].

Teaching methods and curriculum

It was the language specialists' view that the languages programme could be enhanced by making *changes and improvements in teaching methods* and thus having a programme with an *engaging course outline and exciting activities and tasks.* Many (60%) considered the curriculum to be a key factor in improving student motivation and suggested that, coupled with engaging activities that students enjoyed such as games and excursions, making certain that topics were relevant to students' interests, *making links with other areas of the curriculum,* providing students with *more speaking opportunities at higher levels* and *making writing tasks more real or creative* would ensure high-quality teaching and learning and therefore enhance student motivation.

Students' views and perceptions of languages

The student surveys were administered once in the first year of the research and again the following year. In addition to testing the research instruments, the initial data collection aimed to provide us with baseline data, so only 20% of the total numbers in each school was targeted. In the second year of the research the surveys were administered more extensively (Table 3.1). In the account that follows, when two percentages are reported in parentheses, the first relates to the first year of the research and the second to the second year of the study.

Shared views

Although the views of primary and secondary students are for most part reported separately (below), from the analysis of the survey data it was possible to see that they shared a number of points of view.

Table 3.1 Numbers of students who participated in the study

Year levels	First year of study	Second year of study	Totals
Primary			
Year 5	7	72	79
Year 6	8	60	68
Total primary students	15	132	147
Secondary			
Year 7	43	191	234
Year 8	34	132	166
Year 9	11	114	125
Year 10	14	66	80
Year 11	14	17	31
Year 12	–	12	12
Total secondary students	116	532	648
Total students	131	664	795

Very high proportions of both primary (87% | 78%) and secondary students (88% | 84%) agreed that it was good their *school offered languages*; conversely, the proportions of primary (13% | 8%) and secondary students (7% | 5%) who viewed the inclusion of Italian and Japanese in their school negatively were small (the remaining proportions were not certain about this). Further to this, very high proportions of primary (100% | 99%) and secondary students (80% | 90%) remarked that they did *enjoy learning Italian or Japanese*. Although students might have had mixed feeling because *sometimes they enjoyed language but sometime they didn't*, both primary and secondary students commented on the *language programme being enjoyable*. The number of primary students (87% | 74%) and secondary students (56% | 71%) who said they enjoyed languages *sometimes* was higher than the numbers for the other responses. It was also reassuring to see that a fair percentage of primary students (20% | 25%) and of secondary students (35% | 20%) mentioned they *always* enjoyed learning languages. Although the proportion of secondary students who stated they always enjoyed learning a language seems to have decreased in the second year of the study, the number who claimed they *never* enjoyed learning Italian or Japanese remained the same (5%) for both years of data collection.

In terms of *language activities being useful*, the two groups of students held similar views, particularly in the second year of the data collection, when similar proportions of primary (67% | 62%) and secondary (75% | 63%)

felt the activities in their language studies were useful. The percentages of primary students (20% | 28%) and of secondary students (16% | 25%) who were uncertain about this were also similar.

Finally, large proportions of both primary students (14% | 46%) and secondary students (31% | 39%) often did not know whether there were *links between languages and other subjects* and whether the activities undertaken in Italian or Japanese tied in with other areas of the curriculum. However, there were differences here between the two groups, as many of the primary students (80% | 46%) believed there were links, while many secondary students (25% | 33%) believed there were not.

Primary students' views

Primary students were asked to comment on two broad areas: (1) their enjoyment of and achievements in the learning languages; and (2) the language activities they participated in and their usefulness. Overall, students enjoyed learning languages for fun and communication but some found it boring and therefore unenjoyable. Students also felt they tended to do better at receptive rather than productive skills and took part in a range of activities which, because they fostered learning or communication, were seen to be useful. Using the top five terms from primary students, they described Italian and Japanese classes as *fun* because they were *interesting, educational* and also *enjoyable* because they included *games*. Common responses were that learning Italian or Japanese was fun (14% | 15%), it meant they could communicate (14% | 15%), learn another language (40% | 11%) and there was a degree of enjoyment (7% | 10%). Students thought *it was fun to learn a different language* and enjoyed learning Italian or Japanese because their *teacher made activities fun most of the time*, they *played fun games*, they learnt to *speak another language and learnt how to say things*, and they learned *to speak and write and learn about things that [they] can use*.

Students who did not enjoy learning Italian or Japanese most often mentioned that it could be boring (7% | 4%) or difficult (7% | 3%). Their comments seemed to suggest they did not enjoy learning languages because they *didn't find it that interesting*, they *found it boring mostly*, sometimes it was hard *because of the little words* and *it was hard to understand*.

The primary students had mixed views about their skills in receptive or productive language. They thought they did better in writing (80% | 64%) than in reading (67% | 33%) but in the second year of data collection, students' perceptions of their listening skills (60% | 28%) were on par with their speaking skills (40% | 28%).

The students said they participated in a wide range of classroom activities and, although the interest in specific activities varied in the two surveys, students mentioned they would be interested in watching more films or videos (94% | 68%), using computers for a range of purposes (54% | 55%), going overseas (53% | 62%), being involved in cultural activities (53% | 42%) and going to the theatre (40% | 51%). From the list of classroom activities, one that students had expressed no interest in the first survey was cooking (0% | 84%) but this activity recorded the highest percentage in the second collection. When cooking (40% | 40%) was mentioned as an activity that students most enjoyed, the same percentage was recorded in both surveys. The other activities varied between the two surveys in terms of students' preferences so that in the first year of the research the top four activities were computers (34% | 27%), games (40% | 27%), cooking (40% | 40%) and playing games on the computer (34% | 27%) while in the second year the four activities students enjoyed most were excursions (14% | 49%), cooking (40% | 40%), games (40% | 27%) and role-playing (34% | 26%). When reflecting on activities they considered to be ones that promoted language learning and understanding, students were more consistent across the two surveys and identified games (27% | 37%), writing activities (27% | 25%), role-playing (20% | 18%), excursions (14% | 22%) and speaking activities (14% | 18%).

When commenting on the usefulness of language activities, the fact there was learning taking place (40% | 19%) and the fact that language was used for communication (14% | 12%) were the reasons most often given by primary students for why language activities were useful. Whereas some students thought language activities were useful because they *learnt new words* and ultimately *because they could talk to people in that language*, others believed the activities were not useful because the language was not used (7% | 9%) and because they *never had to use it outside school*.

Continuity and transition

When the primary students were asked if they wanted to continue studying Italian or Japanese at secondary school, the proportions who were confident they would do so (40% | 42%) were identical in the first year of data collection and quite close in the second year to the number of students who did not know or were unsure (40% | 46%); only a few students said they would not continue (20% | 12%) with the same language. The main reasons given by primary students for wanting to continue studying the same language related to their knowledge and ability (20% | 9%) and also to the learning (20% | 8%) that had taken place. It was clear these students enjoyed learning Italian and Japanese and *because they had already started they wanted to keep going*, they wanted *to know more* and felt that because they had *already started it would be great to learn more and keep it up*. While a few students thought they *might learn a different language at secondary school*

(7% | 4%), many of the comments made by the students who were uncertain if they would continue studying the same language related to the students moving to a new school (14% | 20%) and being unsure about the languages offered (20% | 9%) *because they did not know if they taught it in their high school*.

Based on the information provided by the secondary students, Italian (64% | 54%) and Japanese (35% | 30%), followed by Indonesian (11% | 7%) at a very distant third, were the languages which students had most frequently learnt in primary school. Because Italian and Japanese were offered in the secondary schools, many primary students could in fact continue their language studies.

When it came to secondary students' recollection of their enjoyment of language at primary school, a higher percentage commented that they had enjoyed languages (59% | 52%) than commented that they had not (39% | 44%). The students who had not enjoyed learning languages at primary school suggested they thought they *didn't learn much* (11% | 9%) and had found learning languages to be *repetitive and boring* (9% | 13%). Another reason why secondary students had either enjoyed or not enjoyed learning languages in primary school was linked to the teacher they had at the time. In the first year of data collection, of those students who commented on the quality of the teacher, 5% stated they *didn't have a good teacher* and exactly the same percentage said they did. In the second year of data collection only 2% of students thought *the teacher made it enjoyable*, while 9% felt that the teacher was responsible for their lack of enjoyment of the subject and thought that their *teacher didn't explain it* or they *never got help when [they] asked for it and the teacher moved on too fast*. This must have been particularly frustrating for one particular student who believed *our teacher never really understood us properly*. Conversely, the comments made by secondary students who had enjoyed learning languages in primary school seemed to indicate they thought it was fun (23% | 15%), interesting (10% | 7%) and activity based (6% | 6%), and thus these students enjoyed learning languages at primary school *because it was always fun and interesting* and included *lots of activities*.

Secondary students' views

The areas secondary students were asked to comment on included: (1) their enjoyment of the subject, (2) language activities and their usefulness, (3) the post-compulsory years, and (4) languages and careers. In general, students liked learning languages. There were many activities they either enjoyed or wanted to see included in the curriculum and, similar to their primary counterparts, secondary students saw as useful activities that fostered learning or communication. These students said their language classes could be *fun* but could also be *boring* and although they could be *interesting, enjoyable, educational* and generally *very good*, they could also be *hard, involve lots of work* which could be *beneficial* but also *challenging*. Even though the numbers of continuing students were greater than the number who did not go on to study the same language at secondary school as at primary, it appeared that going on with the study of languages after the post-compulsory years was not something many students would be doing. Nonetheless, students did identify several jobs where knowledge of a second language would be an advantage. The descriptions that follow include some observations made by secondary students when commenting on the four areas listed above.

In the first year of data collection, the students were not asked whether they liked learning Italian or Japanese. In the second survey, a fair percentage (68%) of students who responded did report enjoying learning language, while a much smaller percentage (17%) did not. In the second year of data collection, many of the comments made by secondary students about why they enjoyed learning languages seemed to suggest that students enjoyed Italian or Japanese because it was fun (16%), interesting (9%) and involved communication (9%). On the other hand, the students who did not enjoy learning languages mentioned that it could be boring or slow (7%), difficult (3%) and also not useful or used (2%).

Secondary students identified many activities they wanted included or increased in the language curriculum. They also listed various activities they had enjoyed in their language classes and recorded a range of activities they believed helped them in learning and understanding languages better. Excursions or trips and videos or films featured prominently in the three lists in both surveys and Table 3.2 lists the top five items (highlighted) in each list in the two surveys.

A fair percentage of secondary students (75% | 62%) deemed language activities to be *useful* because they were learning (20% | 21%) and the activities *help people remember things they learn and understand while they learn two languages*; they could also use the language for communication (10% | 11%) and believed they could be used in the future (6% | 9%) because *you never know when language will come in handy*. A number of secondary students either did not think the activities were useful (2% | 3%) or were not sure about this (5% | 3%) because *some expressions are useful and some aren't* while *some are good and some other are repetative* (sic) and also *sometimes the things [they] do in class don't appear to help and then other things do*.

For the secondary students it was also important to comment on their intentions to continue to study languages in years 11 and 12. Although this was not the case in the first year of the data collection, the number

Table 3.2 Secondary students' perspectives on language activities: Percentages of survey respondents endorsing each activity as most enjoyed, as wanting more of them and as useful for learning and understanding the language

Activities	Activities enjoyed most by students		Would like more of these activities		Activities for learning and understanding	
	First survey	Second survey	First survey	Second survey	First survey	Second survey
Cooking	–	–	–	71	–	–
Computers	10	16	54	48	7	5
Culture	46	38	42	33	7	2
Excursions	42	24	81	69	16	14
Films or videos	37	32	76	72	16	17
Games	32	29	70	69	29	40
Grammar	–	23	–	–	16	7
Listening activities	–	–	44	–	9	14
Oral presentations	25	10	–	–	10	6
Reading activities	11	16	8	9	10	15
Speaking activities	–	19	34	21	23	12
Trips overseas	–	–	62	51	–	–

of students who were intending to continue (81% | 86%) and the ones who were not sure (8% | 38%) were relatively close in the second year. A considerable percentage of students (5% | 20%) said they definitely would not continue with languages past the compulsory years; unfortunately, this group of students seemed quite adamant in their refusal and *they didn't think much would make them study language*. In the first survey, students were not asked to specify why they did or did not intend to continue studying languages past the compulsory years but a range of reasons were given by students in the second survey. The most frequent responses from students who were committed to continuing their language studies included the university entrance score (known as the ENTER score) (8%), enjoyment of or interest in the language (7%) and using the language for communication (6%). These students remarked that *if you studied a language you could get a higher score on your VCE* and that students *enjoyed language they wanted to know fluently another language to perfect that language and speak it fluently*. The students' responses also seemed to suggest they felt confident of their success in VCE. Students who were not sure about continuing with languages in VCE most frequently commented on employment (12%), un-certainties (9%), learning (7%) and academic results (6%). These students suggested they *would have to get a good mark and understand it good* because *enjoying it and doing well* as well as finding out *if it would be useful in their career* would affect their decision. These students also talked about having to make choices which might *collide with more important subjects like English, maths and literature* and ultimately even though it was *important to do a second language ... students could not fit everything in and should do ... what they needed to do to get into the jobs they wanted.*

When it came to thinking about their future and linking language and jobs, although students listed many occupations where knowing another language would be helpful and agreed that knowing Italian or Japanese was likely to help them get a good job, students were somewhat uncertain about what their future career would be and therefore of the importance of Japanese or Italian in relation to it.

Language journals: Language use at school, at home and in the community

Both primary and secondary students were asked to fill in a language journal for a period of two weeks. Students were asked to provide details about which language or languages they used, with whom, where and why. Thus the journals provided a running record of their language use at school, at home and in the community. A hypothetical example is presented in Figure 3.1. There were many instances (78% | 79%) of students using a language that was not English. Not unexpectedly, one activity in which more than a third of secondary students used another language was studying languages or doing homework (40% | 39%). Some students participated in many language activities over the week, others in only a few or none at all. *Speaking* and *studying or completing homework* were also the two activities in which students participated most frequently during the weekend.

Italian and Japanese were the two languages (other than English) most frequently used during the week. Students also used a mixture of English and another language. Although in smaller numbers (45% | 17%) than Italian and/or Japanese, students used a range of other languages, which included Arabic, Chinese, Croatian, French, German, Greek, Hindi, Korean, Maltese, Maori, Norwegian, Spanish, Swedish, Tagalog, Turkish and Vietnamese. Of all the students who used another language, although not in equal numbers, Italian (32% | 16%) and Japanese (23% | 13%) were the two most often used by students during the weekend and, as was the case during the week, students also spoke in a mixture of English and another language and again a range of languages were used.

Students were also asked to provide details about the people with whom they did this activity. During the week, the students who undertook an activity in a language which was not English did it with classmates

Date: Monday 20 March – Sunday 26 March				
Date	Which language?	What did you do?	With whom?	Where? When?
Monday 20 March	Arabic	Spoke on the telephone	My brother	At home In the evening
Tuesday 21 March	Italian	Watched a video (subtitles)	By myself	At school During lunchtime
	Japanese	Did my homework (Reading & Writing)	My friend	At David's place After school

Figure 3.1 Sample language journal

(40% | 39%) or on a smaller number of occasions with the teacher (20% | 23%); they also undertook the activities by themselves (17% | 5%) or with various family members (32% | 29%). During the weekend, the family (50% | 51%) was much more prominent in the list of people students did language activities with and there were very few instances of activities involving the teacher and their classmates (3% | 4%).

In their language journals students also recorded the place and time when the language activities took place. Although many activities took place in the home (41% | 31%), a higher proportion were in the school during the language classes (65% | 64%).

Italian was used at home by 11% of the sample, Japanese by 2%, but many other languages were spoken by the students and their families. The journals illustrated that students used the languages learned at school plus other languages in a range of contexts and for a variety of purposes, varying from *practising for a katakana test with the teacher and the rest of the class*, to *summarising a day in a life of an Italian character* during an Italian lesson, to *listening to mum speak to nonna on the phone*, to watching *Anime in Japanese* or watching *Chilean TV in the evening*, or having a *conversation to nanu in Maltese* or simply saying *hello in Italian with the lollipop man at the pedestrian crossing before going to school.*

The perceptions of and attitudes to language teaching and learning as well as some of the issues raised by students in the surveys and journals were elaborated on and further discussed as part of the focus group interviews. While these interviews provided more in-depth comments on issues students deemed important, Q-methodology was used to extend, analyse and interpret the data to show the shared beliefs and points of view secondary students hold about languages. Both these aspects of the intensive research are detailed in the next chapter.

4   Student Subjectivity

This chapter views the language learning endeavours from the perspective of students, but incorporates the researchers' observations. The data were gathered in focus groups interviews and Q-sorts. The chapter also considers the findings in light of the original core research questions, that is, why the ambitious policies on language education in Australia have met with such uneven success in ordinary schools and with ordinary learners, and aims to identify the perceptions prevailing in schools of the teaching and learning of Italian and Japanese. We are calling this student subjectivity because in a conversation with students one made the point that what 'goes on in my head' is mine. Q-methodology is, in effect, an empirical investigation method for subjectivity, in which the perspectives, categories of understanding and modes of expression of respondents/participants in research are preserved and allowed to organise how the field being researched is understood; that is, they are not structured in advance by researcher categories or templates.

Focus Groups

The intensive research involved only secondary students. A summary of the main themes and some of the comments made by the students in the focus group interviews are presented in this first part of this chapter. Not all of the students responded to every question asked, so it is not possible to provide percentages. The numbers included in the various sections below refer to the number of comments made about specific topics by the participating students. Examples of specific comments made by the students are included and denoted in italics.

Context

A total of five focus group interviews were undertaken at the two secondary schools participating in the research. The focus groups were carried out with small numbers of language students in year 8 at Billabong High School and with small groups of year 9 language students at campuses I and II of River Gum High School. These student years were selected because it is after the completion of year 8 and year 9, at each school respectively, that Italian and Japanese become electives.

During the focus group interviews, students were asked about the Italian and Japanese programmes, the specific curriculum at their school, their feelings about language learning and how languages related to their future, as well as their interests and intended future studies. In addition to providing information about this particular cohort of students, the focus group interviews were used to identify 25 key statements to be used in the research activity involving Q-methodology.

Students and language groups

The language teachers in the participating secondary schools were asked to identify which were the marginal or wavering students and which were the extremely committed language students in their year 8 or year 9 classes. From these groups, a number of students were randomly selected. The aim was to have a total of 30 marginal or wavering students and 30 extremely committed students, that is, 10 students – five learning Italian, five learning Japanese – for each participating school or campus. Unfortunately, not all the students returned a consent form and so only 20 students of Italian and 28 students of Japanese participated in the focus group interviews.

In total, five focus group interviews were carried out. There were two interviews with students of Italian, one at the campus II of River Gum High School and one at Billabong High School; and at each of these sites one focus group interview was also carried out with the students of Japanese.

Table 4.1 Numbers of students who participated in the focus group interviews

	River Gum High School, campus I	River Gum High School, campus II	Billabong High School	Totals
Italian	5	9	6	20
Japanese	10	6	12	28
Totals	15	15	18	48

Because of a number of constraints, the one interview held at campus I of River Gum High School had to include students from both Japanese and Italian language classes. Table 4.1 shows the numbers of students at each school who participated in the focus group interviews.

Languages and learning

Background language

During the interviews, 22 of the 48 students mentioned their language background; while none specified Japanese, six students said they spoke only English and five spoke Italian or *a little bit of Italian* at home. The other 11 students said they spoke another language at home: three spoke Vietnamese and one each mentioned Arabic, Bulgarian, Cantonese, Chinese, German, Greek, Polish and Russian. Although these numbers are low, it appears that background did have a bearing on some of the students' decisions to continue with their language studies (both inside and outside school) and the language students preferred to study.

Language studied at primary school

When students were asked about their prior language learning, 25 stated that in primary school they had studied a different language from the one they were studying at the moment. Eleven indicated that they *did Japanese in primary school* and four of these students did not seem to be happy with the change because, as one student mentioned, *it's hard when you change*. Eight students had been *doing Italian since the start of primary school* but were now studying Japanese. Another six students had studied two languages at primary school, often one being Indonesian. Fourteen students reported they had studied at primary school the same language they were studying at the secondary college. The majority of these students had *done Italian at primary school*, one student who was studying Italian *in primary school …* *did Indonesian and Italian* and the remaining three students *did Japanese in primary school*.

Continue to study languages

When asked if they were going to continue their language study once the subject became an elective, 23 students mentioned that they were intending to do so (that is, they would be or were *pretty sure* they would be studying either Italian or Japanese the following year). One of these students suggested that he would *try to keep going* because his *great-grandmother is Italian* and when he saw her he got *to talk to her a little bit, like, to make her a little bit impressed*.

Seven students commented that they would not continue their language studies. One of these mentioned that he would *rather do other subjects* and he thought that he was *not going to do anything with Japanese*. Another student commented that although she thought that it was *important to do a second language ... [students] could not fit everything in and should do ... [what they] need to do to get into the jobs [they] want.*

Six students suggested that they had not really decided whether to continue their language studies and one of them further commented that the decision depended on *whether [he] found it really easy or really difficult*, while a second student said that she *would like to do it in VCE, it all depends on the progress next year.*

Learning a language outside school

Only four students mentioned they had studied a language outside school but, while one student said that he was *going to be doing Polish in VCE because [he went to] Polish school on Saturdays*, in three cases the student comments seem to suggest that they no longer did so, and they did not specify which language they had learned.

Learning a different language

When the students were asked if there was a language other than Italian or Japanese that they would prefer to learn, quite a number replied affirmatively. Eleven mentioned that they would prefer to study French and of the three students who included a reason for this choice two suggested it was *because [they] just like the culture and it's quite interesting*, while the third had *been to France and just really liked it there and would like to travel there and thought it would be good to be able to speak the language*. Two students mentioned that they would have liked to learn Spanish and the same number stated they would have preferred to learn Chinese. Three students said they would have preferred to learn German and one of these stated this was because he had a German background. Because of his background, Dutch was also mentioned by one student who suggested he *might go to Holland* and had *a big family ... they all speak Dutch and it'd be really cool if [he] could speak it as well*. Maltese was cited by one student *'cause [his] grandpa was Maltese* and one of the students mentioned that he would have liked to learn *Singhalese because [he was] Sri Lankan and [he'd] like to learn about [his] own language*. Other languages mentioned by individual students were Russian and Greek, and Indonesian was identified because the particular student had *gone to Bali and didn't really know Indonesian well*. A couple of students suggested that they would have liked to learn the other language *in addition* to the language they were learning at school and one of the students currently learning Japanese stated that he would *probably learn anything European but probably Italian as a first choice 'cause [he'd] learnt that in primary school.*

Planning for the future

Career

By and large, students had only vaguely formed ideas about their adult careers or about post-school studies (as already evidenced in the data collected through the surveys). One exception was a student who wanted *to become a lawyer and for [him] to get a high ENTER score [he] guessed Italian would have a major impact but [he] didn't want to do Italian but if [he] did it would help [him] a lot but because [he] knew [he] was not good at it [he] was not going to do it.*

Career and language

In trying to get more information about the students' perceptions of the relevance of language to their future, students were asked to picture themselves in 10 years' time. Could they see themselves having a job or a career or doing some extra study or something that involved either Italian or Japanese? Again, students were not certain whether either language would feature in their job or future studies. Eleven were *not sure* or thought that *it might* and one student went further by saying that she'd *been asked this question many times, [she had] absolutely no idea, it might play a role [or] it might not.* Eighteen thought that either Italian or Japanese would feature in their career and when they elaborated their answers seemed to suggest that they felt the language would assist them when communicating with clients, because *when you know how they speak their language it's just better for business to actually engage in their language, they understand better* or, as someone else pointed out, *doctors can talk to patients.* Some of these students also mentioned that a language would help if they had to *work overseas* or *sometimes have to deal with people overseas.*

Thirteen students did not believe Italian or Japanese would be part of their job or future studies. They did *not think [they] would need it* because they *would use just English* in their occupation and did *not think [they] would have a connection to it at all.* Two students stated that, although they did not think Italian or Japanese would feature in their future, *another language* would.

General reflections on the language programme

Before moving on to specific aspects of the language programme, a number of students made comments about the programmes in general.

More students seemed to be happy with the language programme than unhappy, but a number also commented that language did not seem to be a popular or well promoted subject. Specifically, 13 students said that, in the main, they were happy with the language programme. They thought it was, *OK, pretty good* or *not too bad* and one student even suggested he did *not think there was anything wrong with it*.

Five students were very unhappy with the language programme. One suggested that he did *not really enjoy it, [he] found it a waste of time so did not really try for it*, another student simply *hated it*, while another who had *done it since Prep, all the way through [his] schooling had always hated it and thought it was a waste of time* as well.

Students also commented on the popularity of studying a language. Four thought was *not a popular subject*. Interestingly, three who were studying Japanese felt that, in comparison, Italian was a *more popular* subject. Additionally, some students felt that languages were not only unpopular with the students but were not popular, well supported or promoted in the wider contexts of school and community. One student in particular was very articulate and passionate about this. She was committed to learning a language because she thought it was *important to learn a second language* but found it *so hard to learn when the teachers can't control the class*; however, she was *not saying that it was the teacher's fault because the students contribute to that because they don't want to learn it. It's the whole mentality around it. It's not just the class, it's the mentality … teachers, career counsellor and the school as a whole have the mentality that it is only language and they should be promoting every subject the same*.

Improving the language programme

Students were asked what, if they had the opportunity, they would do to improve the Italian or Japanese programme at their school. They proposed many things and their comments could be grouped under a number of broad categories. The largest number of responses mentioned excursions as a way of improving the language programme and changing the type of activities undertaken in the classroom also figured highly. Providing opportunities for communicating with native speakers was seen as something that would enhance the language programmes. Students seemed to have mixed feelings about worksheets. They felt that making language an elective would enhance the synergy in the classroom because only interested students would participate. Trips overseas would lift interest in language and including culture as well as language was important. Students' suggestions are elaborated below and are summarised in Figure 4.1.

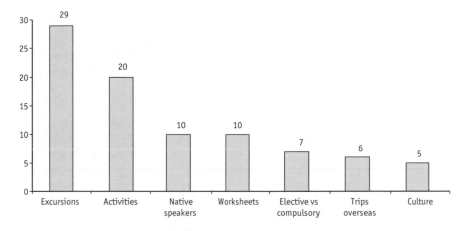

Figure 4.1 Numbers of students in focus groups who suggested ways to improve and promote the language programme

Excursions

Twenty-nine students thought that *an excursion or two wouldn't be too bad* and that teachers could *put in at least one*. Students mentioned that excursions would be *good for knowing about culture and all that stuff*; they would *actually remember more 'cause it's more fun*. *Going out to places* would also provide them with opportunities to *be in the environment, experience it* because they *should incorporate the skills [they] learn in class*. When students kept mentioning restaurants and ordering food, one student suggested that *going to a museum ... art gallery ... going there and actually looking at not just food ... because there is a lot of art* would have been something he would have proposed.

Activities

Twenty students mentioned activities were another area where there could be some improvements to the language programme in their school. Suggestions included *getting out of the classroom and use real-life experiences*, more of *a hands-on approach, more games* or *practical kind of work* such as *cooking food, reading books* or *watching films* or *videos*. These sorts of activities *really helped because even people who did not like [language] contributed to the class*. The idea of *going out somewhere* surfaced again and students clearly liked some variety because they felt they *had been in the same classroom doing pretty much the same work*, which one student thought included *too much theory and [was] too repetitive*.

Native speakers and communication

Ten students talked about the importance of communication and although one of the students thought it was *better to talk one on one with the teacher*, including a range of native speakers in their classrooms was seen as something that would improve the language programme. One student pointed out that *in the classroom there's only one person that can speak proper Japanese so you can only learn from them*, and students thought it would *be better ... to have conversations* and generally *learning how to talk to different kinds of people*.

Worksheets

Ten students commented on worksheets but they seemed to have mixed feelings about them. Five did not seem to like them: they *did sheets all the time* and so suggested either *just stop the worksheets* or *have less worksheets 'cause [they] did not think people really learn through them*. On the other hand, the other five stated that there were *a few worksheets like ... charts and stuff like that worked* because, as one student indicated, *when you are doing a test or something and get to revise you can look back at the sheet and remember things*.

Elective versus compulsory

Seven students thought that language learning would be better if they could *just be able to choose it* so that *the people who really want to learn it can sit there and concentrate properly.* This seemed to suit both the students who wanted to continue and also the students who would *prefer to be somewhere else.*

Trips overseas

Although one of the students thought the school's trip overseas *was not very well promoted and she did not know about it until the beginning of the year*, six stated that sending students on a language overseas trip would lift the interest in the language and, as one student pointed out, by *going to the country they would get to actually be with the people and probably learn better that way.*

Culture

Five students indicated that including culture was important and they could *maybe learn a little bit more about the culture instead of just the language*, as one student pointed out this was *'cause if [they] just learned the language it was not going to help [because] you need to learn a bit about the culture as well to understand their way of life.*

Specific likes and dislikes

During the focus group interviews, students were asked to identify some things they thought were good about the current language programme and also things that perhaps they did not like. Although students were very frank about their dislikes in particular, they were also quite thoughtful in their responses. A little over half of the students commented on the compulsory nature of the programme, while almost as many commented on the types of activities undertaken in class. Together with repetition of topic and content, these seem to be the issues most commented on by the students. The teacher and, almost by default, classroom discipline were also matters on which a good number of students remarked. The other areas on which students commented (in decreasing numbers) included culture, level of difficulty, learning component, communicating with native speakers, relevance and ability levels (Figure 4.2).

Compulsory subject

Students had mentioned compulsory versus elective subjects when discussing ways of improving the language programme and again commented extensively on the advantages and disadvantages of language being a compulsory subject. On the one hand, two students did not seem to mind the fact that language was compulsory for part of the curriculum; one in fact would *rather be forced to do it 'cause there's a lot of subjects* to choose from,

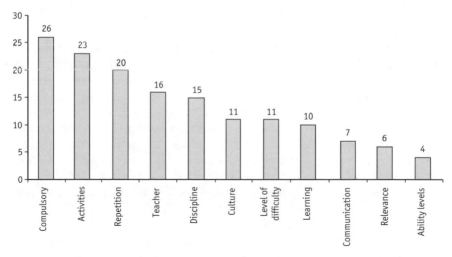

Figure 4.2 Numbers of students in focus groups mentioning their likes and dislikes about language programmes

while the other student suggested that they *should have to do a little bit in year 7 and 8 like [they] do so you know a little bit and so that you don't dislike it before you try it but [she thought] you should get a choice of what you do because if someone has got their mind set on what they want to do and [language] has nothing to do with it, it will just hold you back.* Conversely, 24 students did *not think that language should be compulsory* but rather they *should be able to choose it.* A number of students further commented that the fact that a language was compulsory meant *people [did] not want to learn it because they were forced to* and this in turn led to *a lot of kids [mucking] up in class because they [didn't] want to learn the language* and, furthermore, if the school was *going to make it compulsory ... [students] should have more to choose from not just Italian or Japanese.* Two students also suggested that language becoming an elective would *be a lot easier* and probably *be really good ... because then people who don't want to do it won't be doing it.*

Activities

Activities were something students had discussed extensively when identifying some of the changes they wanted to make to the language programme in their school and they again ranked highly among the specific likes and dislikes. Performances, oral presentations and role-plays were activities the students talked about and generally liked. Six students said *they [liked] doing the role-plays* because they were either *lots of fun* or they liked it *when they [got] marked on them* or they simply *[liked] watching* them. Although one student found *sometimes the activities [got] a bit boring*, four others felt that *[they did] activities ... which make it fun* and, as well as *[being] just fun the sort of activities [they did were] not just all the same.* Two students stated they liked the tests, one because *the tests sort of make you challenge yourself a bit* and the other because he *[liked] to see success.* Another two students indicated that they liked participating in games, like the *little games to help you memorize stuff* or the *games where you flip a card and see the meaning of them and get a score.* Two more students commented they liked *singing the songs*; one suggested she liked performances, specifically *singing the songs because [she] found they stick in [her] head by the tune and stuff.* Individual students also identified some of the things they did not like, One student mentioned he *[did] not like always working from the workbook*, another pointed out that they had *learnt vocabulary ... and grammar*, a third student seemed concerned that *when it came to projects [they] didn't learn anything about it so [they] had to do all this researching*, while a fourth student indicated that *the teaching style ... did not suit [her] and [she didn't] learn [her] best with that style.* Finally, some of the things individual students said they liked included *listening activities* or *drawing.*

Repetition of topics or content

Repetition of topics or content was an aspect about which 20 students made some remark. While one student stated that there was no repetition and the programme was *always different*, 14 pointed out that they *seemed to keep learning the same things over and over again* and *it would probably be better if [they] learnt different things*. Four of these students further commented that they had *learnt the same stuff* in primary school and *every year [they did] kind of the same things*. Five students, however, suggested that *sometimes when [they had] just learned a topic, [the teacher would] go to another topic straight away*, and things could *move along too fast*, so although there might have been repetition, *when [language] was hard it was too fast.*

Teachers

Students made many comments about the language teachers at their school. One concern shared by five students was that in some instances the teachers could *not speak English ... very well so you can't understand*. For some of the students this happened *sometimes*, while one of the students could *not understand what the teacher was saying most of the time*. Seven students, however, mentioned that it was *better to have a Japanese teacher especially in explaining the culture* but also because they could *teach exactly how to pronounce* the words, they could *speak fluently* and also could *explain it a bit better* and, as one of the students mentioned, it *[was] easier to learn Japanese because [the teacher] [knew] everything about it*. Although repetition and pace of the programme were also something that students talked about, four students thought their teacher either *moved on too quickly* or alternatively *might speak too fast*.

Discipline

Fifteen students remarked that there was a discipline problem in the language classes. This was a concern more prevalent with students of Japanese (10 students) rather than with students of Italian. One of the students observed this was *because they were so quiet, the Japanese teachers, they don't really yell at anyone* and another thought *the teachers [were] alright, [they were] just really quiet but that's how Japanese people are*. However, being *so quiet and polite* meant that *the teacher [had] problems controlling the class for the whole time and [students] [got] nothing done, even those who want to learn it [couldn't] do it because other people [were] distracting [them]*. One of the students also mentioned that things could *get pretty disruptive* in the classroom and another pointed out that although she had *learnt a lot, like a fair bit, but not as much as other classes have because ... [the] grade [was] a bit disruptive and [didn't] learn as well as other grades*.

Culture

Eleven students indicated that they *really [liked] learning about their customs and the culture* because they were *interesting* and *different*. The cultural aspects students mainly commented on were the *different customs, food, fashion, traditions* and *celebrations.* What seemed to appeal to the students was the difference between what happened in Italy or Japan and Australia. Again, culture was an area that had previously been mentioned by the students when discussing improvements to the language programme.

Level of difficulty

Eleven students found learning the language was *pretty hard* and it just got *confusing sometimes.* Students commented that *the homework sometimes [was] a bit hard,* the subject *required a lot of revision* and also language *[took] a lot of memorising* and the students found it *sort of hard to remember ... everything.* Some of the students also made remarks about projects and the fact that they were *not really guided so [they didn't] know what to do.* One student seemed to sum it up by saying that with *language you just keep studying, it's one of the ones that really takes a lot of effort.*

Learning

Ten students remarked about the amount of learning they perceived was done in their language classes. These students felt that language classes provided them with *an opportunity to catch up on other work 'cause [they did] nothing,* they did *not learn anything and when [they] learnt something it was boring.* Put simply, these students felt *the whole thing was just a complete bludge.* Some of the students observed that people behaved differently in different subjects even when they were taught by the same teacher and, for example, *everyone [was] paying attention because people actually want to do English* [but] *no one's interested in Italian.* This attitude seemed to occur when, as one student stated, most students who were not intending to continue studying language were *thinking oh well, whatever, I won't do this now, there's only another couple of months and then I'm over and done with it.*

Communication

Communicating, particularly with native speakers, was something the students had made a number of statements about when discussing ways of improving the language programme and this was also mentioned by seven students when discussing their specific likes and dislikes. Four of these students felt it was *better to learn something that actually helped [them] like the basics and how to properly communicate with somebody,* and seemed to like *open discussions to try and improve* their language skills or *real discussions where they don't read cue cards so they can prove that they know how to say the language*. Three students expressed concern about the amount of language they could or, more to the point, could not say and made the observation that they did *not have much of a variety to say anything* or, as one student mentioned, although they could say some things they could *not really express how they really feel 'cause they haven't learned the words yet*.

Relevance

The relevance of language in general or the content taught was something that six students mentioned. Three of these did *not see there [was] much relevance to it*, they *didn't like the fact [they] didn't learn anything they could use* and *believed that [they] should be learning stuff that [they] would use later*. The other three suggested that with *so many subjects ... you should do the ones that you know you need, you like [or] you are good at* and as one of these students observed, this meant *doing something different, not necessarily something better*.

Ability levels

Four students commented on the various ability levels present in the language classes. One student stated that *hopefully [the school] would separate all the people who [didn't] want to do it into different classes so other people could concentrate more* and one of the students suggested that grouping students according to ability levels would be good as he *did not like that there [were] really fluent people in the class that really [knew] their [language] and there [were] people that [weren't] so good like [him]*. The discussion then touched on the number of times topics needed to be taught because of the various levels in the class and the implications of this. One student mentioned that teachers had to *go through a whole week and the first lesson the advanced get it, you know, they'll just get it, then the second lesson the average people will almost get it, then the third lesson, almost the whole class, apart from 2 or 3 people will all get it. But advanced people will just keep on getting it and getting better at it, average people will be pretty good at it; the people that are lacking in [language] skills will be able to catch up a little*. However, as one student pointed out, *people who get it quickly will get bored with it after a while having to keep going over it*. So, *it would be easier*, one student suggested, if students were *put into groups ... and [were] in two separate classes* according to the content they knew or were experts in.

Timetabling

Part of the discussion during the focus group interviews also covered timetabling and time allocation. The ineffectiveness of double periods was a concern raised by the language teachers, so during the interviews students were specifically asked if they had an opinion about double periods compared with single periods. The 10 students who commented on this were in agreement that *unless it's something fun*, double periods were *too long*, they were *boring*, the students got *restless* or they tended to *lose concentration after a while*. While discussing the language timetable, one of the students stated that he would like to *have double the time* given to language studies, and so students were asked how many periods per week, assuming they were only single periods, they thought there should be for Italian or Japanese. The two students who commented on this aspect mentioned that they would increase the number of language lessons to five so that the language could be taught once a day.

Top or preferred subjects

Thirteen students indicated that Italian or Japanese was among their top subjects (Table 4.2), that is, the ones they felt they were doing well in. Of the nine who mentioned Italian, two placed it first on their list, six put it in second place and one listed it third. Four students mentioned Japanese; two of them put it in second place, one in third and the other placed Japanese at number four.

Students were also asked to identify the three subjects they preferred. Twenty students mentioned that either Italian or Japanese was among their preferred subjects (Table 4.3). Fourteen students identified Japanese among their preferred subjects: one student listed it in first place, eight stated it was their second preference and five remarked that Japanese was their third

Table 4.2 Numbers of students in focus groups placing a language among their 'top' subjects

	First place	Second place	Third place	Fourth place
Italian	2	6	1	–
Japanese	–	2	1	1

Table 4.3 Numbers of students in focus groups placing a language among their 'preferred' subjects

	First place	Second place	Third place	Fourth place
Italian	–	3	2	1
Japanese	1	8	5	–

preference. Of the six students who mentioned Italian, three placed it as their second preference, two students as their third and one student said it was his fourth.

Why learn a language?

In the interviews, a number of students remarked on why they thought it was good to learn a language and the main benefits of learning languages (Figure 4.3).

Career

Twelve people mentioned that learning either Italian or Japanese would have benefits as it *opened [their] choices up more for jobs*, it would *look good for the résumé* and would be *particularly important for working overseas*.

Communication

Seven students felt that language would provide benefits in relation to communication, both in Australia and overseas. Using a second language could be of *help in a different country ... if you need to say something to someone*

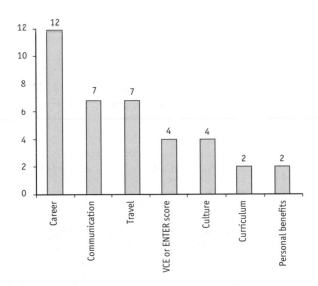

Figure 4.3 Numbers of students in focus groups giving specific reasons why they wanted to learn a language

who didn't understand English, and because *Australia is multicultural ... you can communicate with everyone*. Funnily enough, one student was more interested in other people *not* understanding him and suggested he did *Japanese so [he could] say stuff to [his] sister without her knowing what it means*.

Travel

Seven students mentioned that knowing either Italian or Japanese would be a benefit if *you [planned] to travel in the future* and *if you want to travel around it can just really help*.

VCE or ENTER scores

Only four students suggested that learning a language could be *good for VCE*, and *if [they] did well in it* it enabled students to *get extra marks on [their] ENTER score*.

Culture

Culture was an aspect of the programme that students had previously commented on and four students reiterated that it was *just good to learn another language to understand what other cultures are like*, to *learn about ... other people's beliefs* and *understand their culture better and know when they do something why they do it*.

Curriculum

Two students identified benefits linked specifically to the curriculum. One felt learning language could *help you in other subjects*, for example when learning about the Renaissance in Italian and history, while the student who was learning Greek outside of school suggested that her *Greek helped [her] with [her] Italian ... and [her] Italian has helped [her] with [her] Greek*.

Personal benefits

Finally, two students suggested that learning a language was *kind of challenging* and it *sort of builds character and makes you a bit more unique*.

Q-Study

The comments made by students in the focus group interviews corroborated the survey findings and the interviews provided opportunities for more in-depth discussion. The focus group interviews, however, had a dual purpose – they also provided the 25 statements used in the Q-sort.

Methodology and context

Q-methodology is used to collect, analyse and interpret data to show an individual's beliefs about a particular topic. The statements participants are asked to sort are opinions rather than facts. They are obtained from the discourse which surrounds any topic and need to be rank ordered according to the participant's own point of view.

In the case of this research, the topic students were asked about was the teaching and learning of Italian or Japanese and the comments gathered during the focus group interviews formed the discourse, or concourse, around this topic.

The Q-sample, that is, the 25 statements students were asked to rank, was obtained from the concourse and covered six areas:

(1) teaching;
(2) relevance to the curriculum;
(3) value of learning the language;
(4) classroom control;
(5) organisational aspects of language provision;
(6) learning the language.

The 25 statements were transcribed onto cards and given to the students, who were then asked to make choices and decide how strongly they agreed or disagreed with each statement. To facilitate the sorting activity, students were given a blank grid with a predetermined pattern on which they placed their cards. The symmetrical distribution of the grid meant students had to place three cards in the +3 column ('most like their point of view'), three cards in the –3 column ('least like their point of view'), three cards each in the +2 and –2 columns; four cards each in the +1 and –1 columns, and five cards in the central '0' column. The statements used in the Italian and Japanese Q-sorts, classified by the six areas above, can be found in Appendices 1 and 2, respectively. The nature of the sorting grid will be evident from Tables 4.4–4.9. For convenience, the statements for the Italian Q-sort are also listed under Table 4.4 and those for the Japanese Q-sort under Table 4.7.

When the procedure to be followed in the Q-sort was explained to the students, they were also offered a 'condition of instruction' they could use to guide them in their sorting of the statements. Students were asked to think about a hypothetical situation where they had to describe their language programme to a student who was new to the school and, given this, which were the statements they were most likely to say to them and which were the least likely ones.

Students were also told that, once they had placed all their cards on the grid, they would be given some time to modify the arrangement if they wished, until they were happy that the placement really reflected their own point of view.

The same students who took part in the focus group interviews also participated in the Q-sort (see Table 4.1, p. 84) – 48 marginal or wavering students as well as very committed students in years 8 and 9.

The students were allowed to discuss issues or ask questions of the researchers, who were present during the exercise. The number of participants is typical for a Q-methodology exercise, since the students were working with statements likely to be familiar to them. The results of the Q-sort were analysed using dedicated Q-method software, PCQ; the software allows correlation, computation and factor analysis, and is able to identify the main points of view and shared beliefs in reliable ways.

What follows (for each language separately) is a description of the factors identified by the analysis, the narratives associated with each factor and the most salient differences between each of the language-specific factors. Rather than using the term 'factor', however, in the description and discussion that follow, we have decided to use 'perspectives'.

Sorts and perspectives – Italian

The correlation analysis yielded three perspectives, or points of view, among the students of Italian who participated in the Q-sort. These are recurring statements on which student responses load significantly.

The sort also identified three consensus statements, which are items that have been given the same ranking by the factors. The three consensus statements are:

Statement 1
It's just cool to learn another language.

Statement 2
I learn Italian at school because it seems like a little easier than Japanese because you don't have to learn all those different symbols. It seems easier.

Statement 3
If you learn Italian at a younger age then you'll be able, like, you have more qualifications for a job later in life so, like, it's also an opportunity to … learn … about a different culture instead of just English or Australian.

Table 4.4 Q-sort for Italian perspective 1: *Fix it, but ask us!*

-3	-2	-1	0	+1	+2	+3	*Consensus and distinguishing statements*
4	8	7	3	1	6	17	3 consensus statements:
15	13	12	5	2	16	18	1, 2, 3
24	25	19	10	9	23	20	
			22	11	14		0 distinguishing
			21				statements

1 It's just cool to learn another language
2 I learn Italian at school because it seems like a little easier than Japanese because you don't have to learn all those different symbols. It seems easier
3 If you learn Italian at a younger age then you'll be able, like, you have more qualifications for a job later in life so, like, it's also an opportunity to ... learn ... about a different culture instead of just English or Australian
4 It's good because ... it can also help you in other subjects, like if you learn the history of it and then you could go to history and have got to do stuff on the Renaissance ... and it's great because if you want to travel around it can just really help you
5 Every year we do kind of the same thing in the classes, it's always ... the animals or the numbers and the colours ... you do it pretty much every year, it just goes on from like grade 3 or 4 or something
6 ... if you don't learn the grammar first ... and then start saying sentences you won't understand why some sentences are different to others. And if you don't do the grammar thoroughly first, when you come to year 10, 11, 12, it'll be a real struggle
7 I'd probably chuck out a little bit of the grammar because there's only so much you can take
8 It's an opportunity to catch up on other work 'cause we do nothing in Italian ... you can do your other work in Italian class
9 It's good for an extra mark on your ENTER score
10 It's good to get a chance to learn a European language, if you plan on travelling in the future
11 It's just good cause Australia's multicultural and many people speak Italian so it's good to ... communicate with everyone in Australia
12 There's not much relevance in it, you know, I'd like to learn things which we could use more
13 I don't think there's anything wrong with Italian. I think it's a top subject
14 Well, I did it all the way through primary school and ... I reckon you should be able to select it from year 8 – or year 7 – onwards
15 I haven't learnt anything from Italian ... I seriously have not learnt anything. I've been learning it since like grade 5 or something
16 I'd like to speak to some ... Italian people, that were born there and have come ... and we could like go somewhere where it's all Italian.... Just to get into the Italian way of it and get some food or whatever. 'Cause ... like it's all in the classroom all of it.... We just need to get out of the classroom!
17 I'd have like excursions and stuff, to get out and ... experience it. And maybe read like books and watch films and study more history of Italy than just the language itself
18 They never use computers in Italian. Never
19 ... it'd probably be better like they do it in maths, like extension and stuff, it'd probably be better if they did that in Italian so there's like a group that wants to do like extensions and actually really learn extensively ... to be in one class and people who just want to learn basics in another class ... just get the people that don't want to do it out of the class ... and keep the people that want to do it in the class
20 I reckon they should ask us personally what topics we want to cover and not just set something that no one's interested in
21 I think it'd be better instead of just being asked questions and having answers, if we actually had to have conversations in Italian, so we actually had to be, you know, using Italian, real Italian....
22 It would be better ... if the teacher could actually control the grade....
23 I'd separate all the people who don't want to do it into different classes so the other people could concentrate more
24 It's a bludge and the teachers ... no offence but the teachers, they can't control it
25 The emphasis on learning language should be there from parents, that's where it's got to start, and from the school too. The school offers it but it doesn't promote it and then wonders why we have all these problems ... if everyone had a great aura around Italian, everyone would be enthusiastic ... wouldn't they? Even ... teachers and ... career counsellors and the school as a whole have the mentality that it's 'only Italian'.... They don't promote it to the extent to make people want to do it

Italian – Perspective 1: Fix it, but ask us!

The theoretical Q-sort for perspective 1 is presented in Table 4.4.

In overall terms, perspective 1 is a positive result for the language pro-gramme and for the aims of language policy-makers. It shows a high degree of student confirmation of the aims of the subject in general, and a strong voting down of dismissive statements, such as statements 15 and 24, which were both marked –3, and similarly item 8, which was marked at –2. It is disturbing, however, in terms of programme design, that statement 4, which connects the programme to other subject areas, was marked –3. However, the three highest-ranked statements were calls for improvement (excursions and activities), a lament about pedagogy (failure to use computers in class) and a call for consultation.

Item 25 was marked –2, suggesting a confirmation of the validity of a school-based programme for Italian, rather than a community- or home-based language maintenance activity. Also significant is the collective effect of the +1, +2 and +3 statements. These 10 statements, especially the six at +2 and +3, are an overwhelming endorsement of pedagogical improvement and a call for consultation with learners in programme design. The only mysterious ranking is of statement 13, which is in general agreement with the positive statements that characterise this perspective, but is rated –2.

For these reasons we have labelled the perspective: *Fix it, but ask us!* as this seems to capture the overall feeling of a call for change and a request for greater involvement. Perspective 1 strongly suggests that students want to be able to experience the language through direct activity – excursions, films and cultural activities – and that students want to be involved in the selection of teaching topics. The five statements rated 0, which the condi-tion of instruction suggested 'no opinion, neutral, no strong view', are also revealing. These are statements 3, 5, 10, 11 and 21; two of these, 10 and 11, can be considered slightly political in that they advocate; the others are about programme design and teaching, mirroring aspects made by state-ments rated high (+2 and +3).

There is no statement that categorically distinguishes perspective 1 from the other two points of view identified for Italian.

Italian – Perspective 2: It's a bludge!

Table 4.5 identifies the placement of the statements which characterise the theoretical Q-sort for perspective 2.

Perspective 2 is the opposite of perspective 1. It should be dispiriting for policy-makers and those who invest hope in change, improvement or national aims of the lofty kind we find in policy statements.

Table 4.5 Q-sort for Italian perspective 2: *It's a bludge!*

-3	-2	-1	0	+1	+2	+3	Consensus and distinguishing statements
13	3	4	5	1	2	8	3 consensus statements:
19	6	9	11	14	7	15	1, 2, 3
23	17	10	16	18	12	24	
		21	20	22			3 distinguishing statements: 8, 17, 23
			25				

In this perspective two of the three highest-rated statements are those which perspective 1 ranks lowest. At +3 all three statements are negative about the subject: a major call for improvement in teaching, laments on how little is learned and a condemnation of quality standards (It's a bludge!).

However, the negative rating of statements 23 (calling for streamed classes) and 19 (calling for extension exercises and streaming) and the repudiation of the positive line with no changes needed, statement 13, all rated –3, suggests that aspects that are most strongly representative of this view are that these students see Italian as a subject that entails little or no work because they do nothing and feel they have learnt nothing.

These students clearly do not perceive Italian as a top subject and see no need for streaming and separate classes; however, in the lower ranks of the positive grouping of statements several are relatively positively disposed to the language or the programme.

We have labelled this perspective *It's a bludge!* because this seems to best capture the judgement of the students. This discourse, however, seems to want improvement and its harsh judgement does not appear to call for abandonment of the programme, but rather for drastic revision of how it is designed and delivered.

The three statements that distinguish this from the other perspectives are:

Statement 8
It's an opportunity to catch up on other work 'cause we do *nothing* in Italian … you can do your other work in Italian class.

Statement 17
I'd have like excursions and stuff, to get out and … experience it. And maybe read like books and watch films and study more history of Italy than just the language itself.

Statement 23
I'd separate all the people who don't want to do it into different classes so the other people could concentrate more.

Italian – Perspective 3: They have to back it!

The theoretical Q-sort for perspective 3 is given in Table 4.6.

This perspective makes the point that Italian should be supported by parents and at the school level and is similar in some respects to perspective 1. The highest-rated three statements, 5, 17 and 25, are a criticism of a failure to progress, a call for more active learning and content based instruction (e.g. history) and a call for much more substantial school and family support for the programme. These three link in an interesting way with the three lowest-rated statements: 1, which is an airy affirmation of the value of language study; 4, which claims that the Italian programme supports learning in other subjects (a claim made in statement 17); and 13, which claims that there are no problems in the programme.

These alignments are reinforced by the –2 and +2 statements, confirming a general rejection of statements that imply all is well, or that all is disastrous. Rather, the view seems to be that significant improvement is needed but the school and parents are not particularly serious in their support of the programme. For instance, the students feel there is a lot of repetition in the curriculum.

Because school- and family-backed improvements are felt to be needed, we have called this perspective *They have to back it!*

As well as being a consensus statement, statement 1 is also a distinguishing statement for this perspective.

Table 4.6 Q-sort for Italian perspective 3: *They have to back it!*

-3	-2	-1	0	+1	+2	+3	Consensus and distinguishing statements
1	8	2	3	7	10	5	3 consensus statements: 1, 2, 3
4	14	6	9	12	20	17	
13	18	11	15	19	22	25	
		16	21	23			1 distinguishing statement: 1
			24				

Differences between perspectives – Italian

A number of significant differences were identified between the three points of view.

Most significant differences between perspectives 1 and 2

From Table 4.7 we can see the sharp differences between perspectives 1 and 2: between the discourse of *Fix it, but ask us!* and *It's a bludge!*

The two points of view agree about continuity from primary school and being able to select the subject in secondary school (statement 14, rated 1) and both seem to be neutral about the nature of curriculum content at school and the links between Italian and the community (statements 5 and 11, rated 0).

Italian – Fix it, but ask us!

This perspective suggests students believe that although computers are never used (statement 18, rated +3) there is learning taking place in the classroom (statement 15, rated –3, and statement 8, rated –2) and they do not seem to have concerns about classroom discipline (statement 24, rated –3, and statement 22, rated –1). These students favour a more practical approach to language learning, which includes experiencing the language through excursions, books, films and real communication (statement 17, rated +3, and statement 16, rated +2) as well as being asked about topics of interest (statement 20, rated +3). Students feel there should be separate classes to enable interested people to concentrate on the subject (statement 23, rated +2), they seem to accept grammar (statement 7, rated –1) and realise its importance in the context of continuing with language studies (statement 6, rated +2). Although these students see the relevance of language (statement 12, rated –1) and agree that Italian might help them with their VCE ENTER score (statement 9, rated 1), they may or may not see the links between Italian and future qualifications or future travel (statements 3 and 10, both rated 0).

Italian – It's a bludge!

This point of view conveys the notion that there is no learning taking place in the classroom, even if students have been studying the language since primary school (statement 15, rated +3, and statement 8, rated +3), and that there is little or no classroom discipline (statement 24, rated +3, and statement 22, rated +1). A more practical and experiential approach to language learning does not seem to appeal to these students (statement 17, rated –2) and they do not seem to be interested in being asked about topics

Table 4.7 Differences between Italian perspectives 1 and 2: Between the discourse of *Fix it, but ask us!* and *It's a bludge!*

Negative correlation: 0.30

Item	Statement	Perspective 1	Perspective 2	Difference
15	I haven't learnt anything from Italian... I seriously have not learnt anything. I've been learning it since like grade 5 or something.	−1.788 −3	1.762 +3	−3.550
24	It's a bludge and the teachers ... no offence but the teachers, they can't control it.	−1.329 −3	1.479 +3	−2.808
17	I'd have like excursions and stuff, to get out and ... experience it. And maybe read like books and watch films and study more history of Italy than just the language itself.	2.029 +3	−0.842 −2	2.871
8	It's an opportunity to catch up on other work 'cause we do nothing in Italian ... you can do your other work in Italian class.	−1.063 −2	1.581 +3	−2.644
23	I'd separate all the people who don't want to do it into different classes so the other people could concentrate more.	0.846 +2	−1.306 −3	2.152
6	... if you don't learn the grammar first ... and then start saying sentences you won't understand why some sentences are different to others. And if you don't do the grammar thoroughly first, when you come to year 10, 11, 12, it'll be a really struggle.	1.015 +2	−0.921 −2	1.935

of interest or communicating in and experiencing the language (statements 20 and 16, both rated 0). This perspective expresses the idea that these students do not see the need for separate classes to enable interested people to concentrate more (statement 23, rated −3) and they agree that computers are never used in Italian (statement 18, rated +1). These students favour a less grammatical approach (statement 7, rated +2) as they do not seem to consider it a necessary aspect of language studies (statement 6, rated −2). They do not see the relevance of language (statement 12, rated +2) and do not think it will enhance their job or travel opportunities (statement 3, rated −2, and statement 10, rated −1) nor do they believe it will improve their VCE ENTER score (statement 9, rated −1).

Most significant differences between -perspectives 1 and 3

These two perspectives suggest, although to differing degrees (Table 4.8), that students would like to be asked about topics of interest (statement

3	If you learn Italian at a younger age then you'll be able, like, you have more qualifications for a job later in life so, like, it's also an opportunity to ... learn ... about a different culture instead of just English or Australian.	0.362 0	−1.101 −2	1.464
20	I reckon they should ask us personally what topics we want to cover and not just set something that no one's interested in.	1.522 +3	0.063 0	1.459
7	I'd probably chuck out a little bit of the grammar because there's only so much you can take.	−0.580 −1	0.810 +2	−1.390
12	There's not much relevance in it, you know, I'd like to learn things which we could use more	−0.52 −1	0.834 +2	−1.366
9	It's good for an extra mark on your ENTER score.	0.483 +1	−0.622 −1	1.105
22	It would be better ... if the teacher could actually control the grade ...	−0.676 −1	0.409 +1	−1.086
18	They never use computers in Italian. Never.	1.425 +3	0.378 +1	1.048
10	It's good to get a chance to learn a European language, if you plan on travelling in the future.	0.397 0	−0.653 −1	1.040
16	I'd like to speak to some ... Italian people, that were born there and have come ... and we could like go somewhere where it's all Italian ... Just to get in to the Italian way of it and get some food or whatever. Cause ...like it's all in the classroom all of it ... We just need to get out of the classroom!	0.870 2	−0.134 0	1.004

20, rated +3 and +2) and favour a practical and experiential approach to language learning, which includes excursions, books and films (statement 17, rated +3). Both points of view also denote that students, at this stage, do not see the links between language and other subjects (statement 4, rated –3).

Italian – Fix it, but ask us!

This perspective conveys the notion that learning does take place in the language classroom (statement 15, rated –3), even though computers are never used (statement 18, rated +3). In this perspective, the school is not framed as deficit and it is believed there is support for languages (statement 25, rated –2). These students also realise the importance of grammar in the context of continuing with language studies (statement 6, rated +2) and have no problems with class control and discipline (statement 24, rated –3, and statement 22, rated –1).

Table 4.8 Differences between Italian perspectives 1 and 3: Between the discourse of *Fix it, but ask us!* and *They have to back it!*

Positive correlation: 0.10

Item	Statement	Perspective 1	Perspective 3	Difference
15	I haven't learnt anything from Italian... I seriously have not learnt anything. I've been learning it since like grade 5 or something.	−1.788 −3	−0.038 0	−1.750
18	They never use computers in Italian. Never.	1.425 +3	−0.205 −2	1.630
17	I'd have like excursions and stuff, to get out and ... experience it. And maybe read like books and watch films and study more history of Italy than just the language itself.	2.029 +3	0.538 +3	1.491
20	I reckon they should ask us personally what topics we want to cover and not just set something that no one's interested in.	1.522 +3	0.243 +2	1.279
25	The emphasis on learning language should be there from parents, that's where it's got to start, and from the school too. The school offers it but it doesn't promote it and then wonders why we have all these problems ... if everyone had a great aura around Italian, everyone would be enthusiastic ... wouldn't they? Even ... teachers and ... career counsellors and the school as a whole have the mentality that it's *'only Italian'* ... They don't promote it to the extent to make people want to do it.	−0.894 −2	0.364 +3	−1.258
24	It's a bludge and the teachers ... no offence but the teachers, they can't control it.	−1.329 −3	−0.083 0	−1.245
6	... if you don't learn the grammar first ... and then start saying sentences you won't understand why some sentences are different to others. And if you don't do the grammar thoroughly first, when you come to year 10, 11, 12, it'll be a real struggle.	1.015 +2	−0.152 −1	1.166
4	It's good because ... it can also help you in other subjects, like if you learn the history of it and then you could go to history and have got to do stuff on the Renaissance .... and it's great because if you want to travel around it can just really help you.	−1.377 −3	−0.334 −3	−1.043
22	It would be better ... if the teacher could actually control the grade	−0.676 −1	0.356 +2	−1.033

Table 4.9 Differences between Italian perspectives 2 and 3: Between the discourse of *It's a bludge!* and *They have to back it!*

Positive correlation: 0.10

Item	Statement	Perspective 2	Perspective 3	Difference
8	It's an opportunity to catch up on other work 'cause we do nothing in Italian ... you can do your other work in Italian class.	1.581 +3	−0.265 −2	1.847
19	...it'd probably be better like they do it in maths, like extension and stuff, it'd probably be better if they did that in Italian so there's like a group that wants to do like extensions and actually really learn extensively ... to be in one class and people who just want to learn basics in another class... just get the people that don't want to do it out of the class ... and keep the people that want to do it in the class.	−1.621 3	0.205 +1	−1.826
15	I haven't learnt anything from Italian... I seriously have not learnt anything. I've been learning it since like grade 5 or something.	1.762 +3	−0.038 0	1.800
24	It's a bludge and the teachers ... no offence but the teachers, they can't control it.	1.479 +3	−0.083 0	1.563
23	I'd separate all the people who don't want to do it into different classes so the other people could concentrate more.	−1.306 −3	0.106 +1	−1.412
2	I learn Italian at school because it seems like a little easier than Japanese because you don't have to learn all those different symbols. It seems easier.	1.290 +2	−0.129 −1	1.419
17	I'd have like excursions and stuff, to get out and ... experience it. And maybe read like books and watch films and study more history of Italy than just the language itself.	−0.842 −2	0.538 +3	−1.380
3	If you learn Italian at a younger age then you'll be able, like, you have more qualifications for a job later in life so, like, it's also an opportunity to ... learn ... about a different culture instead of just English or Australian.	−1.101 −2	−0.083 0	−1.018

Italian – They have to back it!

This point of view shows neutrality in terms of the amount of learning occurring in the language classroom and the teacher's ability to control the class (statements 15, 22 and 24, all rated 0). In terms of curriculum, students believe use is made of computers in the language classroom (statement 18, rated –2) and they seem less aware of the importance of grammar (statement 6, rated –1). This perspective also seems to suggest that students perceive a lack of support and status for languages at the school level (statement 25, rated +3).

Most significant differences between perspectives 2 and 3

From Table 4.9 we can see the differences between perspectives 2 and 3: between the discourse of *It's a bludge!* and *They have to back it!*

Italian – It's a bludge!

This perspective conveys the notion that learning does not take place in the classroom and there are issues with discipline (statement 8, 15 and 24, all rated +3). These students do not see the need for separate classes and extension classes (statements 19 and 23, both rated –3) and they perceive Italian as easier language to learn than Japanese (statement 2, rated +2). A more experiential approach to language learning does not seem to appeal to these students (statement 17, rated –2) and they do not think Italian will enhance their future job opportunities (statement 3, rated –2).

Italian – They have to back it!

This point of view articulates the notion that there is learning occurring in the Italian classroom (statement 8, rated –2) and students who do not want to pursue language should not participate in the classes, while the ones who want to learn extensively should be provided with opportunities to do so (statements 19 and 23, both rated +1). The perspective also expresses neutrality regarding the amount of learning occurring in the language classroom, the teachers' ability to control the class and whether Italian provides increased cultural and work-related opportunities (statements 15, 24 and 3, all rated 0). These students do not believe Italian is a softer option than Japanese (statement 2, rated –1) and they favour a more practical approach to language learning which includes experiencing the language through excursions, books, films and history (statement 17, rated +3).

Sorts and perspectives – Japanese

Three perspectives were also identified among the students of Japanese who participated in the Q-sort and there were six consensus statements found.

Statement 2
We should have open discussions to try and improve our Japanese like we just completely talk in Japanese.

Statement 15
Our teacher speaks too fast, and she expects some people already know and sometimes don't and it's disruptive and so some people learn and others don't.

Statement 17
There should be incentives to make people concentrate more.

Statement 19
Like it'd probably be really good next year because then people who don't want to do it, won't be doing it, so ... she'll be able to teach a lot easier.

Statement 22
I'd like to go on more excursions and try the Japanese food and try and make the food too cause I think that would be interesting and, ah, less worksheets 'cause. I think it's better when we sit in a circle and we explain everything as a group. And just, ah, she may ask us a few questions about a certain object an then yeah we answer them and I think that we work better in a group.

Statement 25
The school doesn't really encourage you to do it. But I think it'd be really important like for working overseas and everything plus like ENTER scores at the end of year 12.

Japanese – Perspective 1: Let's use it much more!

The theoretical Q-sort for Japanese perspective 1 is presented in Table 4.10.

This is a perspective of enthusiasm and endorsement for the most part. The aggregated point of view represented in perspective 1 suggests high student interest in Japanese and a belief that there is learning taking place.

Table 4.10 Q-sort for Japanese perspective 1: *Let's use it much more!*

–3	–2	–1	0	+1	+2	+3		Consensus and distinguishing statements
12	9	3	2	4	5	1		6 consensus statements: 2,
14	11	15	7	8	6	16		15, 17, 19, 22, 25
23	13	20	17	10	19	22		
			24	21	18			2 distinguishing
			25					statements: 14, 23

1 I like using the second language because it could help you in a different country if you happen to work there or if you need to say something to someone who didn't understand English
2 We should have open discussions to try and improve our Japanese like we just completely talk in Japanese
3 I like it because we don't do the Japanese on paper and I can't do it on the computer.... Ah, like we're making an advertisement for a car at the moment where we have to use Japanese
4 I really enjoy doing Japanese and like if I want to teach overseas it will be good
5 I like doing Japanese in class when we do things like ... standing up and just talking in conversation with someone, it feels good to know that you can speak in a different language
6 I like Japanese because we learn how to write it in Japanese like using all the characters and stuff ... and ... there's three different types of characters in it. And then I like the teaching 'cause she's like Japanese and then she teaches exactly how to pronounce and which way to say them properly and stuff, yeah
7 Yeah, I'm doing Japanese. It's kind of challenging. More challenging than I think Italian because the letters
8 I do Japanese because I just like their culture
9 I'd have rotating teachers
10 The teaching's good because she's Japanese and she can like explain it a bit better, ah, the activities are easy so that's good and she just uses a lot of Japanese so you get used to it
11 Ah, sometimes you can't really understand her when she's speaking English because she's so used to speaking Japanese and sometimes the activities get a bit boring
12 Sometimes it can be really, really boring and I can't understand what the teacher's saying most of the time
13 I think the teacher moves on too quickly. Like you start one subject and then the next period we'll do another one and then she'll expect us to remember it all
14 I think that 'cause they're so quiet, the Japanese teachers they don't really yell at anyone and they try and control the class, but no one really, a lot of people don't want to be there, there's only about five in our grade that really want to do Japanese
15 Our teacher speaks too fast, and she expects some people already know and sometimes don't and it's disruptive and so some people learn and others don't
16 More activities, more excursions
17 There should be incentives to make people concentrate more
18 We should get more Japanese speakers in our grade and maybe going places where we're like in a Japanese environment and we know what it's like in their culture and their food and everything
19 Like it'd probably be really good next year because then people who don't want to do it, won't be doing it, so ... she'll be able to teach a lot easier
20 I don't think that a language should be compulsory. Like everyone mucks around and it'd be a lot easier if people who really didn't want to do a language could just drop it earlier than year 9
21 I think that we should get people to come in their national dress and also learn a bit more about the culture 'cause we only really learn about the language
22 I'd like to go on more excursions and try the Japanese food and try and make the food too 'cause I think that would be interesting and, ah, less worksheets 'cause I think it's better when we sit in a circle and we explain everything as a group. And just, ah, she may ask us a few questions about a certain object an then yeah we answer them and I think that we work better in a group
23 I think that they should just stop the worksheets altogether because they don't work because people either chuck them out or they just don't do them and then I reckon that they just don't do the work, they just sit there, and do nothing for like a whole lesson
24 I think I might consider teaching English as a second language over in Japan maybe
25 The school doesn't really encourage you to do it. But I think it'd be really important like for working overseas and everything plus like ENTER scores at the end of year 12

There is a consistent call for a more practical approach, which includes excursions, fewer worksheets and activities such as cooking. Students see the usefulness of knowing another language for communication and feel that things will be much better once language becomes an elective and uninterested students no longer participate.

In the overall perspective represented here, statements 1, 16 and 22, which gain the +3 rating, are in two cases are calls for improvement (more excursions) and one a general affirmation; these match well with the three statements ranked lowest, 12, 14 and 23, which effectively repudiate the claims that the programme is boring and that the teachers are too quiet and in insufficient control, and reject worksheets. However, of most interest here is that four of the six lowest-ranked statements (14, 11 and 13, and also partly 9) are criticisms of the teachers, specifically the native Japanese teachers (they are unable to maintain class discipline, are too quiet, cannot engage students or move too quickly), and all these are rejected with student ratings of –3 or –2. Two of the positively rated statements are also direct supports for the teachers (10 and 18), while another are strong indications of support for Japanese language and culture. Statement 19, rated +2, confirms this general pattern and anticipates even more improvement when the language becomes an elective rather than compulsory subject. Statement 1, rated +3, is a 'good citizen' type of affirmation and confirms the policy settings which imagine a wider cultural and attitudinal value of language study. We have called this perspective *Let's use it much more!* because this seems to capture both the enthusiasm that is represented in the sorting pattern and the call for some improvements.

Two statements distinguish perspective 1 from the other two points of view for Japanese:

Statement 14
I think that 'cause they're so quiet, the Japanese teachers they don't really yell at anyone and they try and control the class, but no one really, a lot of people don't want to be there, there's only about five in our grade that really want to do Japanese.

Statement 23
I think that they should just stop the worksheets altogether because they don't work because people either chuck them out or they just don't do them and then I reckon that they just don't do the work, they just sit there, and do nothing for like a whole lesson.

Table 4.11 Q-sort for Japanese perspective 2: *I'm not following you!*

−3	−2	−1	0	+1	+2	+3	Consensus and distinguishing statements
3	7	5	2	1	19	13	6 consensus statements: 2, 15, 17, 19, 22, 25
8	21	11	4	6	20	14	
9	24	12	15	10	23	22	2 distinguishing statements: 8, 13
		17	16	18			
			25				

Japanese – Perspective 2: I'm not following you!

Table 4.11 shows the theoretical Q-sort for the Japanese perspective 2.

This point of view suggests strong concerns about the pace and content of teaching Japanese. The six highest-rated statements (i.e. those scored +3 and +2) are like appeals for help. Statements 13 and 14 are here rated opposite to how they were rated in perspective 1 (at −3 and −2). For perspective 2, these mutually reinforcing claims for teaching improvement were given the top marked scores, along with statement 22, with its call for a more active, less classroom-focused teaching practice. Statements 13 and 14 link directly to statements 19 and 20, which identify compulsion as a problem for Japanese. Statement 23 ties to statement 22 as a pedagogical claim, but the other four top-rated statements all concern a desire to be able to follow the teacher better and for a more transparent practice of teaching.

We have called perspective 2 *I'm not following you!*, to reflect this sense of bewilderment. Statement 14 also contains the idea that some of the students who loaded onto this perspective are waverers and are unlikely to continue to study Japanese, and the more committed ones appear to be looking forward to their departure.

Two statements distinguish perspective 2 from the other two points of view for Japanese:

Statement 8
I do Japanese because I just like their culture.

Statement 13
I think the teacher moves on too quickly. Like you start one subject and then the next period we'll do another one and then she'll expect us to remember it all.

Table 4.12 Q-sort for Japanese perspective 3: *No compulsion!*

-3	-2	-1	0	+1	+2	+3	Consensus and distinguishing statements
3	5	2	6	1	12	16	6 consensus statements: 2, 15, 17, 19, 22, 25
4	10	9	7	8	14	20	
24	18	13	11	23	19	22	
		21	15	25			0 distinguishing statements
			17				

Japanese – Perspective 3: No compulsion!

Table 4.12 presents the theoretical Q-sort for perspective 3.

Although there are no statements that distinguish perspective 3, this view makes the point that Japanese should not be compulsory and these students also want to be able to participate in more activities and excursions. There appears to be a degree of boredom and these students do not seem to enjoy Japanese. This student perspective brings together statements19 and 20 (rated +2 and +3), which express a wish to have removed from class those unwilling to do the subject, and 16 and 22 (both rated +3), which express a wish for a more active pedagogy. These are, however, linked to statements 12 and 14 (both rated +2) and cast an overall slightly negative sense over perspective 3, but its main message seems to be that compulsion should be removed, and so this is the name we have given the perspective: *No compulsion!*

Differences between perspectives – Japanese

A number of significant differences were identified between the three points of view as outlined in Tables 4.13–4.15 and summaries.

Most significant differences between perspectives 1 and 2

Japanese – Let's use it much more!

This perspective rejects the idea that, because of their background, Japanese teachers are unable to control the class and a large number of students are not interested in learning the language (statement 14, rated –3). It denotes enjoyment in the use of a second language for communicative purposes both outside the classroom (statement 1, rated +3) and within it (statement 5, rated +2). Like all others, these students see the benefits of excursions, practical activities, oral activities and group work (statement 22, rated +3) but they also want to have more activities and excursions

Table 4.13 Differences between Japanese perspectives 1 and 2: Between the discourse of *Let's use it much more!* and *I'm not following you!*

Positive correlation: 0.08

Item	Statement	Perspective 1	Perspective 2	Difference
14	I think that cause they're so quiet, the Japanese teachers they don't really yell at anyone and they try and control the class, but no one really, a lot of people don't want to be there, there's only about 5 in our grade that really want to do Japanese.	−1.612	0.368	−1.980
23	I think that they should just stop the worksheets altogether because they don't work because people either chuck them out or they just don't do them and then I reckon that they just don't do the work, they just sit there, and do nothing for like a whole lesson	−1.457	0.250	−1.707
16	More activities, more excursions.	1.628	0.051	1.576
13	I think the teacher moves on too quickly. Like you start one subject and then the next period we'll do another one and then she'll expect us to remember it all.	−1.008	0.478	−1.486
11	Ah, sometimes you can't really understand her when she's speaking English because she's so used to speaking Japanese and sometimes the activities get a bit boring	−1.426	−0.066	−1.360
12	Sometimes it can be really, really boring and I can't understand what the teacher's saying most of the time.	−1.457	−0.110	−1.347
5	I like doing Japanese in class when we do things like...standing up and just talking in conversation with someone, it feels good to know that you can speak in a different language.	1.085	−0.221	1.306
1	I like the using second language because it could help you in a different country if you happen to work there or if you needed to say something to someone who didn't understand English.	1.372	0.140	1.232
8	I do Japanese because I just like their culture.	0.465	−0.581	1.046

(statement 16, rated +3) and they do not think that the worksheets should be phased out because students do not engage with them (statement 23, rated –3). At this point, the students do not find Japanese boring (statement 12, rated –3, and statement 11, rated –2) and they do not seem to have problems understanding the teacher or with the pace of the lesson (statements 11 and 13, both rated –2, and statement 12, rated –3). This point of view also suggests that, as well as culture, there are other things students enjoy (statement 6, rated +2, and statement 8, rated +1).

Japanese – I'm not following you!

This view expresses concerns about the pace at which material is presented and also teachers' expectations (statement 13, rated +3). Students experience some boredom and are, at times, unable to follow what is being presented in Japanese (statement 12, rated +2, and statement 11, rated 0). Japanese culture holds no appeal for these students (statement 8, rated –3) and they feel that the teacher's background is a reason for their inability to maintain discipline and affects the number of students who want to be in the class (statement 14, rated +3). These students do not seem particularly interested in increasing the number of activities and excursions (statement 16, rated 0) and being able to communicate in a range of situations holds a little appeal for them (statement 1, rated +1); they are not too keen on some of the communicative activities in the classroom (statement 5, rated –1) and believe that worksheets do not hold students' interest or engage them in learning (statement 23, rated 2).

Most significant differences between perspectives 1 and 3

Japanese – Let's use it much more!

This perspective suggests students reject the notion that Japanese teachers, because of their background, are unable to control the class and that a large number of students are not interested in learning the language (statement 14, rated –3) but concedes, as do the students endorsing the other perspectives, that things will be easier for the teacher once uninterested students are no longer learning Japanese (statement 19, rated +2). These students are able to understand the teacher, do not feel Japanese is boring (statement 12, rated –3, and statement 11, rated –2) but rather enjoy it (statement 4, rated +1). They do not think that the worksheets should be phased out because students do not engage with them (statement 23, rated –3) and they enjoy the communicative type of activities that occur in the classroom (statement 5, rated +2) but they also see the links between language and the world outside the classroom (statement 4, rated 1). All students disagree with the idea of having rotating teachers and this group feels strongly about this (statement 9, rated –2). The students would like to see an increase in the number of activities and excursions (statement 16, rated +3), they enjoy the use of a second language for communicative purposes and the benefits it may provide (statement 1, rated +3) and the perspective suggests these students are more at ease with the use of the target language by the teacher (statement 10, rated +1).

Table 4.14 Differences between Japanese perspectives 1 and 3: Between the discourse of *Let's use it much more!* and *No compulsion!*

Positive correlation: 0.08

Item	Statement	Perspective 1	Perspective 3	Difference
14	I think that cause they're so quiet, the Japanese teachers they don't really yell at anyone and they try and control the class, but no one really, a lot of people don't want to be there, there's only about 5 in our grade that really want to do Japanese.	−1.612	0.177	−1.789
12	Sometimes it can be really, really boring and I can't understand what the teacher's saying most of the time.	−1.457	0.270	−1.727
23	I think that they should just stop the worksheets altogether because they don't work because people either chuck them out or they just don't do them and then I reckon that they just don't do the work, they just sit there, and do nothing for like a whole lesson	−1.457	0.156	−1.613
11	Ah, sometimes you can't really understand her when she's speaking English because she's so used to speaking Japanese and sometimes the activities get a bit boring	−1.426	−0.021	−1.405
9	I'd have rotating teachers	−1.426	−0.021	−1.405
5	I like doing Japanese in class when we do things like...standing up and just talking in conversation with someone, it feels good to know that you can speak in a different language	1.085	−0.227	1.312
16	More activities, more excursions.	1.628	0.383	1.244
1	I like the using second language because it could help you in a different country if you happen to work there or if you needed to say something to someone who didn't understand English.	1.372	0.163	1.209
10	The teaching's good because she's Japanese and she can like explain it a bit better, ah, the activities are easy so that's good and she just uses a lot of Japanese so you get used to it.	0.798	−0.326	1.125
19	Like it'd probably be really good next year because then people who don't want to do it, won't be doing it, so ... she'll be able to teach a lot easier	1.271	0.199	1.072
4	I really enjoy doing Japanese and like if I want to teach overseas it will be good.	0.636	−0.411	1.047

Japanese – No compulsion!

This perspective suggests these students agree with the idea that, because of their background, Japanese teachers are unable to control the class and that a large number of students are not interested in learning the language (statement 14, rated +2). These students do not really enjoy Japanese nor do they see its potential for future employment (statement 4, rated –3, and statement 1, rated +1). They do not seem to enjoy some of the communicative classroom activities (statement 5, rated –2), they think worksheets do not really engage students and should be stopped (statement 23, rated +1) and, as the students endorsing perspective 1, would like to see the number of activities and excursions increased (statement 16, rated +3). At times, this group finds Japanese and some of the activities boring and have difficulty understanding the teacher (statement 12, rated +2); they are non-committal about the teacher's use of English (statement 11, rated 0) but feel that being a native speaker does not mean the explanations are better nor that hearing the target language regularly makes it easier (statement 10, rated –2). This group, like the others, disagree with the idea of having rotating teachers (statement 9, rated –1) and concur that things will be easier for the teacher once uninterested students are no longer learning Japanese (statement 19, rated +2).

Most significant differences between perspectives 2 and 3

As there were no differences with values >1.0, Table 4.15 reflects the top five differences:

Table 4.15 Differences between Japanese perspectives 2 and 3: Between the discourse of *Let's use it much more!* and *No compulsion!*

Positive correlation: 0.44

Item	Statement	Perspective 2	Perspective 3	Difference
8	I do Japanese because I just like their culture.	–0.581	0.177	–0.758
13	I think the teacher moves on too quickly. Like you start one subject and then the next period we'll do another one and then she'll expect us to remember it all.	0.478	–0.206	0.684
9	I'd have rotating teachers	–0.581	0.021	–0.597
10	The teaching's good because she's Japanese and she can like explain it a bit better, ah, the activities are easy so that's good and she just uses a lot of Japanese so you get used to it.	0.162	–0.326	0.488
4	I really enjoy doing Japanese and like if I want to teach overseas it will be good.	0.074	–0.411	0.485

Japanese – Let's use it much more!

This point of view suggests that Japanese culture holds no appeal for these students (statement 8, rated –3) and they are concerned about the pace at which material is presented and about the teacher's expectations (statement 13, rated +3). All students disagree with the idea of having rotating teachers and this group feels strongly about this (statement 9, rated –3). These students feel that having a teacher who is a native speaker means explanations are better and that hearing the target language regularly makes it easier (statement 10, rated +1) but they are not sure about their level of enjoyment of the subject or its links with the world of work (statement 4, rated 0).

Japanese – No compulsion!

This perspective implies that Japanese culture holds some appeal for these students (statement 8, rated +1) but also seems to suggest students do not really enjoy Japanese, nor do they see its potential for future employment (statement 4, rated –3), although they have fewer problems with the pace at which topics are presented and the expectations of their teacher (statement 13, rated –1). Like other students, they disagree with the idea of having rotating teachers (statement 9, rated –1) and feel that being a native speaker does not mean the teacher's explanations are better, nor that hearing the target language regularly makes it easier for them (statement 10, rated –2).

General Observations from the Data

The Q-data and to a lesser extent the focus group and survey data presented in this volume offer compelling evidence of how students 'talk back' to policy. In Chapter 1 and partly in Chapter 2 we traced the world and the worldview of policy-makers. In this universe the objects of attention are national and international legitimations for issuing policy texts. These texts take the form of official declarations of what is wanted and expected of the nation's future citizens. In general, they are to be able to engage with multicultural realities through the use of language skills and insight. Australia's present priority is economic and regional engagement in Asia, and so the key languages of commerce in the region – Chinese, Indonesian, Japanese and Korean – feature strongly in the new projected vision of Australia. The multicultural elements of language policy have secured a strong presence for Italian in schools too.

Policy declarations are statements of intent. They are debated and negotiated in the media and elsewhere. A process of policy interpretation seeks to refine and sharpen what policy should aim to achieve, how it should be designed, what its priorities ought to be and how it should be implemented. The present volume considers how implementation is seen by students. This is a radical shift from the more usual focus. It makes it clear that students are active in forming opinion and in speaking back to the part of the policy implementation system they encounter: teachers, schools and fellow students.

The overall impression from the data is that there is a broadly positive response to the aims of policy documents, both the multicultural response and Asia literacy, but the biggest impression from the discourses of the students is that they do not consider their learning experiences positively or likely to succeed. The students, many of them in both languages, are calling for more systematic and higher-quality language learning. We argued in Chapter 2 that policy implementation should be considered part of a continuum of the making of policy and this perspective is supported by the evidence presented in this chapter. The lofty aims of policy declarations ride uneasily on such generally reflective students and while many are waverers perhaps the majority are committed, or would be, if the language programmes offered were more rigorous and active.

5 Pushing Policy To Be Real

During 2012 and 2013 Australia 'went retro' in its language policy, essentially recalling visions and plans of the mid-1980s about Asian engagement and Australian redefinition, and a new phase of vigorous public discussion on language policy was initiated. The tone and content of much of this discussion was set by the remit the Prime Minister allocated to the commission that produced the White Paper on *Australia in the Asian Century* (Australian Government, 2012). With its origins in Prime Ministerial authority, and marked discursively by strong ties to the national interest, and characterised by trade and security concerns, there is little conceptually innovative or original in its prescriptions. The White Paper says little about transnationalism, mobility or cosmopolitanism as the new contextual ground for language education and contemporary communication. These visions and perspectives reside in other domains; the official vehicles for language policy debate were set in the original framing and its mainstream reaction. On 24 January 2012 the current affairs programme *The 7:30 Report*, produced by the Australian Broadcasting Corporation (ABC), went to air with a story entitled 'Language lessons languish in Aussie schools'. The account of language learning in the programme is set from the presenter's opening statement and is a perfect mirror of much of the debate: 'Asian language education across the Australian school system is in catastrophic decline' (ABC, 2012; see also Group of 8, 2007). We might question the claim that there has been a 'catastrophic decline', as a dispassionate look at the statistics shows that this characterisation is rather extreme. Nonetheless, the shape of a considerable part of language planning is prefigured in the interaction between such crisis language of the ABC report, and the priorities, assumptions and tone of the White Paper. It will be difficult for nuance to be introduced into a field of discussion marked by its urgency, where language teaching is tied to the highest needs of the nation, and which has drawn the participation of the highest political representatives in the land. This means that the teaching of foreign languages, and especially some Asian languages understood as foreign to Australians but critical for national economic and political fortunes, is seen as an issue of unarguable urgency. Indeed, one of the participants in the ABC programme suggested that in present circumstances Australian children need to learn Chinese, and that this was the first time Australians had ever needed to learn another language (understanding language learning as always connected to foreign places and others).

From a language planning perspective it is clear what the relationship will be between the official text which has emerged as the White Paper, declaring the policy 'intention', and the debate and discussion, which are being channelled towards full approbation of language study, centring on who the learners are seen to be, the choice of languages and what measures will be set in place to overcome the 'catastrophic decline'.

What is far less clear, though history provides some guide, are the implementation and likely effects of the policy set out in the White Paper. Some of the sharply critical reaction cited in Chapter 1 suggests that many critics have given up on public education. Some now promote large-scale in country exchanges (Lane, 2013a, 2013b) and others suggest reliance on the language skills of immigrant Asians (Herscovitch, 2012b, 2013a).

The policy is a continuation of Australia's recent style of forceful, top-down language planning, informed by little reflection on the exact causes of the 'catastrophic decline'. Accepting the reality of the decline (if perhaps questioning its degree), three causes could be posited:

(1) unwarranted political interference in language learning – but in fact all sides share the general aims of 'Asia literacy' and tend to compete instead simply over who is best placed to 'deliver';
(2) lack of funding – but while funding has been lower than it should have been, the more relevant point is that the specific languages suffering 'catastrophic decline' are the only ones for which dedicated funding, to quite high levels, has been provided, ever since 1994;
(3) lack of engagement on the part of one or more sections of the community – but teachers have not opposed language teaching (despite some opposition from primary school principal associations some years ago, this was minor and temporary, and not targeted at specific languages, and in any case was essentially a call for more support to implement language programmes rather than in principle opposition to their teaching); and neither have parents (though the majority of parents accept that languages could be or are beneficial for students' careers).

To what, then, are we to attribute this 'catastrophic decline'?

The Canadian Council on Learning (2009) produced a brief document summarising the state of knowledge about successful 'large scale educational reform' (p. 2). Hoping to direct changes in education, especially in 'the way schools operate', to avoid the large costs involved, or to make the large-scale investment successful rather than wasteful of taxpayers' money, the document looked at 'reorganizing entire school systems, rather than implementing individual school improvement initiatives' (p. 2). As with most reflections of this kind, the focus was on student achievement and many of the messages stressed the long-term nature of change, as well as the critical importance of 'concurrence and involvement' of teachers and of others 'responsible for implementation'. It argued that 'comprehensive educational reform programs can be much more effective than more targeted initiatives that are focused more narrowly'. This comment was directed at meeting the needs of students at risk of school failure, but much of what the document stated is consistent with other research. For instance, a US meta-study (Borman et al., 2003), looking at 232 individual research projects on innovation and change, highlighted the critical role of 'ongoing' teacher professional development and 'acceptance' and 'buy-in' of the reform programme by those implementing it directly and others linked to them in professional circles.

So far we can see from these lines of reasoning the crucial role of approaching large-scale change in educational contexts by paying attention to what we will call an 'ecology' of effects, whereby no innovation or change can be quarantined from other parts of the system being reformed and the whole-hearted participation of those affected, and those around those affected, are important ingredients in success. Michael Fullan is a specialist researching leadership in educational change and the 'culture' of change. He has examined many cases of successful and failed innovation or change in education from different parts of the world. In a reflection on the role of government in effecting change, Fullan (2001) distils three generalisations. These can be seen as the broad strategies available to government, such as those central authorities in Australia that want to invigorate Asian language teaching. Public authorities, or 'government', essentially have at their disposal three broad options for effecting change. They can seek to bring about change by: (1) imposing accountability (system-wide or targeted); or (2) providing incentives (either 'negatively', as pressure, or 'positively', as support); or (3) directing their attention towards 'capacity-building' for key agents in the field being addressed, such as teachers, schools or universities. 'Capacity-building' involves not merely 'training up' teachers to be technically competent in the tasks required, but also gaining their commitment to the objectives and need for the innovation. Fullan's case is that it is rare to find a judicious combination of the three: governments typically opt for one, stressing accountability or imposing incentives, and that, because of the nature of education as an activity devolved to professional specialists, and occurring in relationships between teachers and learners, the third broad strategy is of fundamental importance, but too often ignored.

Thus, educators and education researchers tend to highlight and notice the importance of involving professionals, either the teachers required to deliver the innovation being considered, or the teachers and other professionals associated with those teachers. However, languages are not like other subjects. Languages have communities of speakers who identify with and support the language, whose communicative behaviours, outside of school control or central policy prescription, make a critical difference to the policy process. This wider ecology is an important element in whether central language plans, the intentions of policy-makers, attain success. Specifically related to language education we can cite Tollefson (2002), who stresses the importance of school and community relationships in language education innovations. He looks at state-mandated and centralist policies in diverse settings and asks about the relationship of these to local aspirations for language rights and the recognition of languages that might not enter the state's prescription of what is important for learners to study. The tensions that are thrown up in such cases highlight the need for democratic practices in language policy-making.

In Australia, the policy proposals in 2012 were practically identical to those in 1994. It is possible, therefore, or even highly likely, that the policy will produce the same effects. An authoritative official text declaring policy intention based on a clear depiction of the national interest will, as we see with the ABC programme, engender a supportive discourse and public debate, and possibly, as we saw in Chapter 1, a nuanced rebuttal (e.g. Slattery, 2007), and no doubt also a more vigorous rebuttal (e.g. Price, 2011; and the citizen bloggers), but central top-down prescription will prevail and increases in resources will be deployed, which are of course welcome and needed. However, this is a well trodden path. More disturbing are the prospects for real and lasting change. Such tenacious Australian language planning, at least since 1991, has been decreasingly democratic and increasingly desultory in its effects (Lo Bianco, 2001).

In previous chapters we have seen how deep the gulf between policy-making and policy implementation can be and therefore how a theory of social change, for instance as envisaged by Cooper (1989), is more complex than is often imagined. Ambitious policy-makers often become impatient with calls for consultation and long-term and systematic planning. They see problems that need tackling and are liable to interpret calls for 'hastening slowly' as obstruction. Worse, many of these voices from the top interpret the claims to language rights, minority language maintenance, and other ways to view language policy and practice, as unnecessary complications, or naïveté, or as hostility. One of the authors (Lo Bianco, 2008) noted at a major American language planning conference hosted jointly by the US Department of Defense and Department of Education a dismissive tendency by non-language specialists to assert that 'solving' the language problem was not 'rocket science'. And yet, they could not explain continuing systemic failure to 'solve the problem'. Real-world language policy-makers, those in positions of power and authority, sometimes imagine that the failure of educational systems in English-speaking countries to achieve the goals of language policy is the result of ill will or opposition, stupidity or ignorance among the implementers and that drawing up language policies is not a specialist skill with a discrete body of concepts and experience. As a result they rarely draw on the skill of language planners, or the research evidence and concepts of language planning theory.

Continuing policy failure, however, should make advocates more modest. They lack tools and their ideas lack traction in key domains where they are implemented. This is surely not simply because the mechanisms of accountability or incentives are lacking, but also because the conversations of inclusion have been neglected. There is much need of capacity-building, but there is need of much else as well. Teachers and students generally (in the present study, mostly students) are calling for involvement, to improve and enhance programmes, to which, despite their rather trenchant criticisms, they are committed. Teachers and students may seem to be the least powerful link in the 'language planning policy' chain we have been describing, but even half-heartedness from them is potentially devastating for language policy goals. If teachers and (especially) students withdraw interest, withhold commitment, deny enthusiasm to the purposes of language policy by 'failing to learn', then authoritative official texts, Prime Ministerial White Papers and vigorous public discourse are made vulnerable to 'catastrophic decline'.

It is clear from this discussion that language policies do fail not solely because they lack full endorsement at the junctures where they should be implemented. They can also fail if, in those junctures, there is only half-hearted support. Because language learning (and use) involves substantial change to the person concerned – a new way to see the world, new behaviours, new value systems, new stocks of knowledge, new conversational partners, new conversational routines, new ways of being present as a human subject in the world – it differs significantly from other fields of study. Languages are both timetabled subjects in school curricula and lived codes of communities. Entering those communities requires emotional, intellectual and pragmatic acceptance of many (perhaps most) of the norms that prevail there. This 'new order of things' (as Machiavelli put it) requires deep change and commitment, and is vulnerable even with the support of 'lukewarm defenders'. A new enterprise must both recruit support and build capacity for its enactment, and this must be dispersed across multiple semi-autonomous fields of action. One of these is those at the furthest end of the process: students.

It is a salutary lesson for the central makers of language education policy that the act of policy dispersal may jeopardise its implementation; nonetheless, sharing its aims is not merely desirable but essential for success, as our data clearly show. The enterprise will be endangered by a failure to understand, as the evidence shows, the deep curriculum changes required, the extensive effort needed and the systemic changes implied in those policy aims. The benefits of learning another language and the cumulative nature of language learning are not generally understood, and this itself becomes a factor. It makes policy feel 'unreal' in those settings, colloquially but appropriately called 'on the ground', where things really matter. This represents a clear case in which the depictions of power in old prescriptions of language planning theory falter. Our research shows how even the apparently subjugated, minor and ephemeral power conceded to the implementers – teachers, students and administrators in schools – by the voices that produce the declarative texts of language policy is, in the end, a major and material power. The power to withhold enthusiastic support is itself sufficient to thwart the ambitions of the nation-makers, if the teacher and the student conserve their interactions of learning as an autonomous domain.

An awareness of this is seen in prescriptions (invariably phrased in contemporary management speak) about involving stakeholders and ensuring collaboration. However, these usually appear like nostrums, moral injunctions about the 'right' way to do things. Language education policy depends on 'stakeholders' and 'collaboration' in a more material and concrete way.

At least some generalisations emerge from these findings that should be recorded here. New language programmes are accompanied by nation-making ideologies and grand ambition but policy-makers need to devote more serious thinking to the ways in which language education plans are promoted, especially the claims that are made for the benefits of learning languages. In particular, there must be a more concerted effort to respond to concerns in the general community about academic achievement and English literacy. This failure to be fully committed to serious programmes – on the part of principals, teachers other than language teachers, administrators, some parents and students – is a drag on implementing the kinds of programme that will yield greater proficiency in languages.

The kinds of language teaching that attracts the interest of students involves content from other discipline areas, and this suggests the deep need for cross-faculty collaboration at school level. This, too, is likely to be regarded as desirable rather than essential. Content-based programmes, or scenario-based language teaching at least, are critically important to even the most minimal proficiency gains. Such programmes diversify, enrich and enliven the experience of language teaching and learning and, in conjunction with full-immersion (for example well designed language retreats), promote improved acquisition and authentic communication.

Policy should support languages staff and teachers from other disciplines in the planning and delivery of collaborative, content-based instruction and specific pedagogical shared activities. The aim is authentic communication. In the present study this perception was shared by some teachers from other disciplines who identified possible areas of collaboration and integration across the curriculum, but without larger numbers doing this the enterprise will remain superficial and remote from the attainment of the high-end goals espoused by policy-makers. More critical even than the perceptions of the academic staff (both those directly involved in language teaching and those not so directly involved but who control other disciplines and access to them) are, of course, the perceptions of learners. The data show how important student perceptions of language education are, how much they can see through the pretence often put up by schools, teachers, administrators and Prime Ministers. Their judgements and the level of their commitment need to be taken seriously and incorporated in programme design. That design should incorporate opportunities for motivated and talented individuals to undertake work at rates and with content appropriate for them; and adaptation for those learners who are less committed to learning a language and who require differentiated content. This latter point poses considerable difficulties for schools and educators, since many see this as academic streaming and resist its implications.

A more straightforward conclusion comes from the question of continuity. The chopping and changing endemic in Australian language education needs to stop for effective improvements to take hold. The data show that students continuing to study the same language learnt at primary school are concerned about repetition of content. This leads to boredom and the feeling that little learning is occurring, which in turn fuel cynicism about policy and its aims. We could group all the questions that arise here under the term 'transition'. Since the education experience is segmented, as a result of the organisational and conceptual arrangements of bureaucracies and the professional personnel employed in them, transition becomes a question of more than simply administration. There are any number of practical means for overcoming this problem, from portfolio links across school levels to much more personalised practices of education centred on individual learners and their pathways. These, however, serve only to provide a record of learning undertaken by students; what is more important than this is continuous teaching, or at least harmonised teaching. The record of learning needs to shape the next phase teaching. Too often secondary teaching assumes that nothing valuable has occurred at primary school, and while this might be deleterious for all subjects, language teaching critically depends on cumulative and sustained engagement, and is especially badly affected by poor transition planning. At this point transition itself transitions from being a question of administration to becoming an obstacle for language education planning. In a more philosophical sense, however, the 'transition problem' involves links between home and school, between one set of language experiences and the schooled ones, and not just the sectoral divisions that have been exposed in the data.

What can be seen reasonably consistently in the evolution of Australian language policy is that successive policies seem to be designed to achieve less than their predecessors do. A recent volume edited by Liddicoat and Scarino (2010) shows that despite constant revisions to and developments of policy, the aims have become lowered and limited, rather than refined and expanded. Instead of elevating practical achievements, policy has instead been narrowed, even as its stated aims have expanded or become more ambitious, what it finances has become more modest and anodyne.

This is clear when comparing the two major policy reports on Asian languages, both championed by Kevin Rudd. Although addressing the same four languages, constituted as the (foreign) languages of the strategic and commercial partners of Australia, and therefore in the foreign interest, the 1994 Rudd report aimed for widespread and lasting change, including for a proportion of 60% of language candidates taking these four Asian languages (40% for all other languages), and for this enterprise to take place within a widespread Asia literacy curriculum revolution. The programme was sustained for eight of its intended 10 years and, although estimates of the funding allocated vary a little, from over $240 to $290 million (vast sums in the Australian budget context), depending on whether matching state grants are counted, its second incarnation as the National Asian Languages and Studies in Schools Program (NALSSP) aimed to have fewer students study the targeted languages. While the NALSSP specified proficiency outcomes, these were widely held to be unachievable and unrealistic, because of the much reduced financing and the programme's short duration. This latter problem entrenches the damaging perception among 'implementers' that policy-makers have little knowledge of the problems and realities of schooling, the world of learners and teachers. The replacement of all this effort with the overarching claim of the 2012 White Paper that all students will have 'access' to Chinese, Hindi, Indonesian or Japanese does little to foster optimism in realistic language planning.

The problem besetting these aims is best described by reference to Indonesian, which, because of romanisation of its orthography, geographic proximity, and large number of teachers trained over several decades, should enjoy stronger standing in Australian education than it does. Despite both the National Asian Languages and Studies in Australian Schools (NALSAS) strategy and the NALSSP, and with the prospect of things being radically different unlikely under the White Paper, headlines such as 'Plan unable to save study of Indonesian' (Lane, 2011) still regularly appear, in which the usual headline inflation is no exaggeration. Lane's article states: 'Murdoch University Indonesianist David Hill, who has been looking for ways to revive the language, said the 2007 NALSSP policy was "an empty gesture if the government is not prepared now to provide the necessary resources to support the teaching of such languages"'.

The designers of language education policy do not directly control all the relevant domains and settings where their aims are to be implemented and this makes the enterprise difficult, at the least, to plan. Other aspects of language policy have similar qualities, so that changing the way a community speaks its language, or adopting orthographic reforms, is beset by the unique quality of language, which is that its users have ultimate control over its use. Policy designers can and do gain traction over language in diverse ways, and the education system remains the most likely mechanism for enactment of policy, but even here, as we have seen, there are limits to the traction that policy can achieve. If policy aims were restricted to questions of participation in school programmes, and the kinds of programmes to be delivered, language education policies would seem more pragmatic and realistic. However, they typically merge with cultural, identity, attitudinal, economic, social and national aims whose attainment is much more difficult to achieve and describe.

The end result of language education must involve some level of knowledge of a second language. This, at least, is the test required in the court of public opinion, among learners in schools, and in the media and public discussion. For most practical purposes, in Australia Japanese is a foreign language. In our study, few learners had any background proficiency in Japanese or any non-school contact with the language. Students studying Japanese in an Australian-Japanese community would be studying an extension of their language of home communication. Inevitably this would be a language with some local norms and characteristics. We see the absence of the real world in the overwhelming criticism by the students, exemplified in Japanese discourses *Let's use it much more!*, *I'm not following you!* and *No compulsion!* (see Chapter 4). Sometimes schools try to replicate aspects of real-world communication but there is only a superficial similarity between the tasks learners are engaged in at school and 'real' communication in another language. Lived languages involve students in comparing what appears on the timetable and what exists in domains of communication outside school, so they notice differences in culture, emotion and norms of use, and often face challenges to their identity from these disparities.

The position of Italian in light of directions of public policy for 2013 and beyond is more complex. It has a secure place within the national curriculum, but it lacks the state endorsement that has benefited Japanese and that will continue under the White Paper. On the other hand, Italian benefits by having a vigorous community of interest. The evidence from our study of discourses in schools shows that the implementation domain, the transmission system outside the home, is fragile and weak. The student interest is strong, but the programmes are academically weak. The students want the schools and teachers to *Fix it, but ask us!* This is a call for improvement, in terms of both quality and rigour. The students decry the programmes, saying *It's a bludge!* But they do not mean by this that they enjoy the fact that the programme demands little of them. The Q-sort evidence is clear: the students are demanding a more rigorous programme. Finally, the students are claiming that *They have to back it!* Again, this should be a cause for celebration: the students are not saying in the face of what they interpret to be poor provision that the programme should be terminated. Instead, they are demanding improvement.

In the translation of policy ambitions into practice there is a radical change in the actors involved and different domains of action, each with its unique discourses. Policy-makers see themselves serving the national interest and believe this national interest transcends local needs, as well as local differences of perception or opinion. The national interest as decided by opinion-makers, public servants and diplomats can seem an abstract and far-away notion in classrooms. In contrast, the continuum of language policy in fact spans a series of relatively autonomous domains. Different actors, with overlapping agency, initiate, interpret, endorse or subvert language policy in their particular settings. Each set of actors is constrained by different stocks of information and knowledge, is pressured by different constituencies, makes do with different rationalisations and compromises, and, although they appear to be unequal in power and voice (the politician and the teacher, the administrator and the parent, the teacher and the student), such differences in overt and formal power are not sustained across all the domains. Past assumptions about who is to be considered a language planner and where language planning occurs cannot be sustained. Instead, language planning is revealed to be a continuous (practically seamless) activity, with multiple points of potential disruption and subversion, enacted at different levels of intervention, which are usually unreconciled and sometimes contradictory.

The asserted realities of policy rhetoric contrast with the actual realities in schools; student judgements of the effectiveness of different learning arrangements contrast with policy depictions; the statistical depictions of policy-makers and advocates map uneasily on to the lives of learners. These 'lives' are themselves complicated by the actual and the imagined, by the current and the anticipated. This is the key theme of the volume: constant iteration between school and nation, policy and practice. It should form the basis for a wide-ranging reflection on language planning practice and ultimately a contribution to answering the question: *Is a theory of language planning possible?*

We need to ask the question to understand why, as the new millennium proceeds, Australia, a wealthy, privileged, first-world state, geographically placed at the edge of Asia, integrating economically and increasingly socially into that region, a multicultural and multilingual country *par excellence*, with mostly efficient and effective institutions, general public calm and formally democratic procedures of governance, still struggles with language education. It has singularly failed to institute language management and planning procedures that are appropriate to its current and future needs and that are desired and demanded by the majority of its citizens. This odd, even bizarre state of affairs is not unique to Australia: Britain and the United States, at least, share Australia's low-ambition language policies.

Untangling this conundrum is worth undertaking, not merely to throw light on the specifics of Australia's language planning experience, but also more widely, since it asks about the complexities of language policy-making, about English in the world, about multilingualism and even about how we cling to outdated ideologies of monolingual institutional life despite the reality of more complex plurilingual states forged in the increasingly integrated context of globalisation.

Specifically in relation to the students we have worked with over the period of this study, and the policies we have examined, Italian and Japanese represent about half of all students involved in the public effort for languages. The unique histories of the two languages tell much of the story of Australia's experimentation with national reconstruction through language education. Some of this seems naïve, some heroic, some misguided, some dispiriting, but most of it commendable and sincere. The admirable, impressive and often bewildering sequence of policies, the intense debates, arguments and differences of opinion on which the policies reside, the two worlds, Asia and Europe, Japanese and Italian depict will remain vibrant and permanent features of all discourse on projects of planning Australian communication.

We can only hope that a new phase of language policy can be initiated, though this looks unlikely at present. The national interest cannot be seen to exclude the rights of minorities and different perceptions of how an agreed national interest is to be pursued. Australian language education policy rightly stresses the critical importance of national integration into Asia and the practical and pragmatic challenges this integration poses. But there are many reasons for learning languages, there are many kinds of 'capital' represented by language knowledge, there are many communities that identify with their own languages but who are still Australia's citizens. It is surely odd to foster a notion of the national interest that excludes the interests of many in the nation, and it is surely in any conception of the national interest to foster cultural democracy and fairness. It is practically possible and historically demonstrated that more ambitious and more egalitarian policies are feasible.

The improvements we are encouraging should be introduced into the process of language planning, which needs to be more democratic in its style and more inclusive in its conversations, at the three levels of language planning that we have been discussing: policy intention, policy debate and policy implementation. Admitting more voices into policy discussions will on its own stimulate language planning which is more representative of the totality of the nation's multiple communication needs and language problems. It will also improve quality of programmes, because those closer to implementation and language use can influence their design and content. Such changes will certainly need to embrace both Japanese and Italian, the Asia and Europe these languages have represented in the historic phases of Australian language policy, and of course other languages: the foreign languages and community languages Australians want to learn, as well as Australian languages – the Indigenous languages that are still spoken in determined resistance to the almost incomprehensible failure to support them within public education. Such a wider policy remit and more inclusive spirit succeeded in the past, when Australia's language policy was in the forefront of world language planning, and could succeed again in the future.

Appendices

Appendix 1: Q-Statements, Italian

> T Teaching (classroom level) (5)
> R Relevance of the curriculum (4)
> V Value of learning the language (5)
> C Classroom control (2)
> O Organisational aspects of language provision (school level) (4)
> L Learning the language (general) (5)

L 1 It's just cool to learn another language

L 2 I learn Italian at school because it seems like a little easier than Japanese because you don't have to learn all those different symbols. It seems easier

V 3 If you learn Italian at a younger age then you'll be able, like, you have more qualifications for a job later in life so, like, it's also an opportunity to ... learn ... about a different culture instead of just English or Australian

V 4 It's good because ... it can also help you in other subjects, like if you learn the history of it and then you could go to history and have got to do stuff on the Renaissance ... and it's great because if you want to travel around it can just really help you

R 5 Every year we do kind of the same thing in the classes, it's always ... the animals or the numbers and the colours ... you do it pretty much every year, it just goes on from like grade 3 or 4 or something

R 6 … if you don't learn the grammar first … and then start saying sentences you won't understand why some sentences are different to others. And if you don't do the grammar thoroughly first, when you come to year 10, 11, 12, it'll be a real struggle

R 7 I'd probably chuck out a little bit of the grammar because there's only so much you can take

T 8 It's an opportunity to catch up on other work 'cause we do nothing in Italian … you can do your other work in Italian class

V 9 It's good for an extra mark on your ENTER score

V 10 It's good to get a chance to learn a European language, if you plan on travelling in the future

L 11 It's just good cause Australia's multicultural and many people speak Italian so it's good to … communicate with everyone in Australia

V 12 There's not much relevance in it, you know, I'd like to learn things which we could use more

L 13 I don't think there's anything wrong with Italian. I think it's a top subject

O 14 Well, I did it all the way through primary school and … I reckon you should be able to select it from year 8 – or year 7 – onwards

I 15 I haven't learnt anything from Italian … I seriously have not learnt anything. I've been learning it since like grade 5 or something

T 16 I'd like to speak to some … Italian people, that were born there and have come … and we could like go somewhere where it's all Italian…. Just to get into the Italian way of it and get some food or whatever. 'Cause … like it's all in the classroom all of it…. We just need to get out of the classroom!

R 17 I'd have like excursions and stuff, to get out and … experience it. And maybe read like books and watch films and study more history of Italy than just the language itself

T 18 They never use computers in Italian. Never

O 19 … it'd probably be better like they do it in maths, like extension and stuff, it'd probably be better if they did that in Italian so there's like a group that wants to do like extensions and actually really learn extensively … to be in one class and people who just want to learn basics in another class … just get the people that don't want to do it out of the class … and keep the people that want to do it in the class

T 20 I reckon they should ask us personally what topics we want to cover and not just set something that no one's interested in

T 21 I think it'd be better instead of just being asked questions and having answers, if we actually had to have conversations in Italian, so we actually had to be, you know, using Italian, real Italian….

C 22   It would be better ... if the teacher could actually control the grade....

O 23   I'd separate all the people who don't want to do it into different classes so the other people could concentrate more

C 24   It's a bludge and the teachers ... no offence but the teachers, they can't control it

O 25   The emphasis on learning language should be there from parents, that's where it's got to start, and from the school too. The school offers it but it doesn't promote it and then wonders why we have all these problems ... if everyone had a great aura around Italian, everyone would be enthusiastic ... wouldn't they? Even ... teachers and ... career counsellors and the school as a whole have the mentality that it's 'only Italian'.... They don't promote it to the extent to make people want to do it

Appendix 2: Q-Statements, Japanese

T	Teaching (classroom level) (12)
R	Relevance of the curriculum (1)
V	Value of learning the language (3)
C	Classroom control (3)
O	Organisational aspects of language provision (school level) (3)
L	Learning the language (general) (3)

V 1   I like using the second language because it could help you in a different country if you happen to work there or if you need to say something to someone who didn't understand English

T 2   We should have open discussions to try and improve our Japanese like we just completely talk in Japanese

T 3   I like it because we don't do the Japanese on paper we do it on the computer.... Ah, like we're making an advertisement for a car at the moment where we have to use Japanese

V 4   I really enjoy doing Japanese and like if I want to teach overseas it will be good

T 5   I like doing Japanese in class when we do things like ... standing up and just talking in conversation with someone, it feels good to know that you can speak in a different language

L 6   I like Japanese because we learn how to write it in Japanese like using all the characters and stuff ... and ... there's three different types of characters in it. And then I like the teaching 'cause she's like Japanese and then she teaches exactly how to pronounce and which way to say them properly and stuff, yeah

L 7 Yeah, I'm doing Japanese. It's kind of challenging. More challenging than I think Italian because the letters

L 8 I do Japanese because I just like their culture

O 9 I'd have rotating teachers

T 10 The teaching's good because she's Japanese and she can like explain it a bit better, ah, the activities are easy so that's good and she just uses a lot of Japanese so you get used to it

T 11 Ah, sometimes you can't really understand her when she's speaking English because she's so used to speaking Japanese and sometimes the activities get a bit boring

T 12 Sometimes it can be really, really boring and I can't understand what the teacher's saying most of the time

T 13 I think the teacher moves on too quickly. Like you start one subject and then the next period we'll do another one and then she'll expect us to remember it all

C 14 I think that 'cause they're so quiet, the Japanese teachers they don't really yell at anyone and they try and control the class, but no one really, a lot of people don't want to be there, there's only about five in our grade that really want to do Japanese

T 15 Our teacher speaks too fast, and she expects some people already know and sometimes don't and it's disruptive and so some people learn and others don't

T 16 More activities, more excursions

C 17 There should be incentives to make people concentrate more

T 18 We should get more Japanese speakers in our grade and maybe going places where we're like in a Japanese environment and we know what it's like in their culture and their food and everything

C 19 Like it'd probably be really good next year because then people who don't want to do it, won't be doing it, so ... she'll be able to teach a lot easier

O 20 I don't think that a language should be compulsory. Like everyone mucks around and it'd be a lot easier if people who really didn't want to do a language could just drop it earlier than year 9

R 21 I think that we should get people to come in their national dress and also learn a bit more about the culture 'cause we only really learn about the language

T 22 I'd like to go on more excursions and try the Japanese food and try and make the food too 'cause I think that would be interesting and, ah, less worksheets 'cause I think it's better when we sit in a circle and we explain everything as a group. And just, ah, she may ask us a few questions about a certain object an then yeah we answer them and I think that we work better in a group

T 23   I think that they should just stop the worksheets altogether because they don't work because people either chuck them out or they just don't do them and then I reckon that they just don't do the work, they just sit there, and do nothing for like a whole lesson

V 24   I think I might consider teaching English as a second language over in Japan maybe

O 25   The school doesn't really encourage you to do it. But I think it'd be really important like for working overseas and everything plus like ENTER scores at the end of year 12

References

ABC (2012) 'Language lessons languish in Aussie schools', *The 7:30 Report*, broadcast 24 January.

ABC Lateline (2009) 'Deputy opposition leader Julie Bishop joins Insiders to discuss the outcomes of the G20 meeting in London', broadcast 5 April 2009, from http://www.abc.net.au/insiders/content/2009/s2535196.htm.

ABS (2006) A picture of the nation, 2070. http://www.ausstats.abs.gov.au/ausstats/subscriber.nsf/LookupAttach/2070.0Publication29.01.0910/$File/20700_Cultural_overview.pdf. Retrieved 2 June 2013.

ABS Ancestry (2013) Cultural diversity in Australia. http://www.abs.gov.au/ausstats/abs@.nsf/Lookup/2071.0main+features902012-2013. Retrieved 2 June 2013.

AEF (2010a) *The Current State of Chinese, Indonesian, Japanese and Korean in Australian Schools: Four Languages, Four Stories*. Melbourne: Asia Education Foundation.

AEF (2010b) 'Asian languages education crisis deepens. report shows', press release, 26 May, from http://www.asialink.unimelb.edu.au/__data/assets/pdf_file/0005/419990/asian_language_crisis260510.pdf.

Asialink and Asia Society Austral-Asia Centre (2011) 'Don't drop Asia in schools: business urges government, press release, 30 March (with letter, 16 March 2011), from http://cms.unimelb.edu.au/__data/assets/pdf_file/0011/438842/Dont_drop_Asia_studies_and_languages.pdf.

Australia 2020 (2008) *Australia 2020 Summit: Initial Summit Report*. Retrieved 12 January 2012 from http://www.safecom.org.au/pdfs/2020summit-initial-report.pdf.

Australian Embassy (2011) *Australian Embassy Rome News*, 4 July, from http://www.italy.embassy.gov.au/files/rome/Australian%20Embassy%20Rome%20Newsletter_Issue%204_July%202011.pdf.

Australian Government (2012) *Australia in the Asian Century*. Canberra: Commonwealth of Australia, from http://asiancentury.dpmc.gov.au/sites/default/files/white-paper/australia-in-the-asian-century-white-paper.pdf.

Australian Institute for International Affairs (2013) 'McCarthy, Wesley attack Asian white paper', Australian Institute for International Affairs, NSW, blog, 25 February, from http://glovercottages.wordpress.com/2013/02/25/mccarthy-wesley-attack-asian-white-paper.

Beeson, M. and Jayasuriya, K. (2009) The politics of Asian engagement: Ideas, institutions, and academics. *Australian Journal of Politics and History* 55 (3), 360–374.

Bellocchio, L. (2006) *Anglosfera. Forma e forza del nuovo Pan-Anglismo*. Genova: Il Nuovo Melangolo.

Bennett, J. (2004) *The Anglosphere Challenge: Why the English-Speaking Nations Will Lead the Way in the Twenty-First Century*. Lanham, MD: Rowman and Littlefield.

Borman, G., Hewes, G., Overman, L. and Brown, S. (2003) Comprehensive school reform and achievement: A meta-analysis. *Review of Educational Research* 73 (2), 125–230.

Bourdieu, P. (1991) *Language and Symbolic Power*. Malden, MA: Polity Press.

Brown, S.R. (1980) *Political Subjectivity: Applications of Q Methodology in Political Science*. New Haven, CT: Yale University Press.

Brown, S.R. (1993) A primer on Q methodology. *Operant Subjectivity* 16 (3–4), 91–138.

Burnley, I.H. (2001) *The Impact of Immigration on Australia: A Demographic Approach*. South Melbourne: Oxford University Press.

Byram, M. and Risager, K. (1999) *Language Teachers, Politics and Cultures*. Clevedon: Multilingual Matters.

Byram, M., Lapkin, S., Lo Bianco, J., Met, M. and Scott, A. (2010) Fremdsprachendidaktik in englischsprachigen Ländern. In W. Hallet and F. Königs (eds) *Handbuch Fremdsprachendidaktik* (pp. 28–35). Hannover: Friederich Verlag.

Callick, R. (2011) Crusade for China literacy. *The Australian*, 21 May, from http://www.theaustralian.com.au/news/world/crusade-for-china-literacy/story-e6frg6ux-1226059888990.

Canadian Council on Learning (2009) *Changing Our Schools: Implementing Successful Educational Reform*, from http://www.ccl-cca.ca/pdfs/LessonsInLearning/01_15_09-E.pdf.

Cha, Y-K. and Ham, S-H. (2008) The impact of English on the school curriculum. In B. Spolsky and F. Hult (eds) *The Handbook of Educational Linguistics* (pp. 313–328). London: Blackwell.

Chesterman, J. and Galligan, B. (eds) (1999) *Defining Australian Citizenship: Selected Documents*. Canberra and Melbourne: National Archives of Australia and Melbourne University Press.

Church, J. (2005) *Per l'Australia: The Story of Italian Migration*. Victoria: Miegunyah Press.

COAG (Council of Australian Governments) (1994) *Asian Languages and Australia's Economic Future*. Brisbane: Queensland Government Printer.

Commonwealth of Australia (2008) *Australia 2020 Summit, Final Report*. Canberra: Department of the Prime Minister and Cabinet, from http://apo.org.au/sites/default/files/2020_summit_report_full.pdf.

Cooper, R. (1989) *Language Planning and Social Change*. Cambridge: Cambridge University Press.

Corson, D. (1999) *Language Policy in Schools: A Resource for Teachers and Administrators*. Mahwah, NJ: Erlbaum.

Davis, K. (1994) *Language Planning in Multilingual Contexts: Policies, Communities, and Schools in Luxembourg*. Philadelphia, PA: John Benjamins.

Dawkins, J. (1991) *Australia's Language: The Australian Language and Literacy Policy*. Canberra: Australian Government Printing Service.

de Mejía, A-M. (2002) *Power, Prestige and Bilingualism International Perspectives on Elite Bilingual Education*. Clevedon: Multilingual Matters.

Department of Education, Employment and Workplace Relations, *Reports on the State of Asian Language Education in Australian Schools*, from http://deewr.gov.au/reports-state-asian-language-education-australian-schools.

Department of Immigration and Multicultural Affairs (2001) *Immigration: Federation to Century's End, 1901–2000*. Canberra: Department of Immigration and Multicultural Affairs, from http://www.immi.gov.au/media/publications/statistics/federation/federation.pdf.

De Swaan, A. (1993) The evolving European language system: A theory of communication potential and language competition. *International Political Science Review* 14 (3), 241–255.

De Swaan, A. (2004) Endangered languages, sociolinguistics, and linguistic sentimentalism. *European Review* 12 (4), 567–580.

Douglas, W. (1994) 'Trionfo' in Ingham. The Italian community in north Queensland. *Studi Emigrazione* 113, 43–64.

Department of Prime Minister and Cabinet (2011) *Australia in the Asian Century* (Issues Paper). Department of Prime Minister and Cabinet, from http://asiancentury.dpmc.gov.au.

Duranti, A. (2007) *Etnopragmatica. La forza nel parlare*. Roma: Carocci Editore.

Economist (2008) The Manchurian candidate. The ideological convergence of Australia and Japan. *The Economist*, 11 June, from http://www.economist.com/node/11527400?story_id=11527400.

Elkner, C., Martinuzzi-O'Brien, I., Rando G. and Capello, A. (2005) *Enemy Aliens: The Internment of Italian Migrants in Australia*. Ballan: Connor Court.

Favero, L. and Tassello, G. (1978) *Cent'anni di emigrazione italiana (1876–1976)*. Roma: Centro Studi sull'Emigrazione Cser:

Fishman, J. (2001) *Can Threatened Languages Be Saved? Reversing Language Shift Revisited: A 21st Century Perspective*. Clevedon: Multilingual Matters.

Fitzgerald, S. (1997) *Is Australia an Asian Country?* Sydney: Allen and Unwin.

Freebody, P. (2007) *Literacy Education in School: Research Perspectives from the Past, for the Future* (AER 52). Camberwell: Australian Council for Education Research.

Fukuyama, F. (1992) *The End of History and the Last Man*. New York: Free Press.

Fullan, M. (2001) Governments. In *The New Meaning of Educational Change* (4th edn) (pp. 219–236). London: Cassell.

Galbally, F. (1978) *Migrant Services and Programs: Report of the Review of Post-arrival Programs and Services for Migrants*. Canberra: Australian Government Publishing Service.

Gillard, J. (2011) Speech to the Asialink and Asia Society Lunch, Melbourne. http://www.pm.gov.au/press-office/speech-asialink-and-asia-society-lunch-melbourne.

Goad, P. (2004) *Melbourne Architecture*. Boorowa: Watermark Press.

Grattan, M. (2011) White paper to proceed on tippy-toes. *The Age*, 29 September, from http://www.theage.com.au/opinion/white-paper-to-proceed-on-tippytoes-20110928-1kxg7.html.

Group of 8 (2007) *Languages in Crisis: A Rescue Plan for Australia*. Canberra: Group of 8 Universities, from http://www.go8.edu.au/__documents/university-staff/agreements/go8-languages-in-crisis-discussion-paper.pdf.

Gumperz, J. and Hymes, D. (1972) *Directions in Sociolinguistics: The Ethnography of Communication*. New York: Holt, Rinehart and Winston.

Harries, O. (1993) Clash of civilisations. *The Weekend Australian*, 3–4 April, p. 19.

Harrison, D. (2011) Business in plea on Asian languages. *The Age*, 31 March, from http://www.theage.com.au/national/education/business-in-plea-on-asian-languages-20110330-1cgcw.html.

Heller, M. (ed.) (2007) *Bilingualism: A Social Approach*. Basingstoke: Palgrave Macmillan.

Herscovitch, B. (2012a) Half-baked language policy is al dente, 2 November. Sydney: Centre for Independent Studies, from http://www.cis.org.au/publications/ideas thecentre/article/4601-half-baked-language-policy-is-al-dente.

Herscovitch, B. (2012b) Australia's Asia literacy non-problem (Paper 133), 5 September. Sydney: Centre for Independent Studies, from http://www.cis.org.au/images/stories/issue-analysis/ia133.pdf.

Herscovitch, B. (2013a) Language policy gone loco, 1 February. Sydney: Centre for Independent Studies, from http://www.cis.org.au/publications/ideasthecentre/article/4689-language-policy-gone-loco.

Herscovitch, B. (2013b) Australia and the Asian ascendancy: Why upskilling is not necessary to reap the rewards (Issue Analysis 137), 19 February. Sydney: Centre for Independent Studies, from http://www.cis.org.au/publications/issue-analysis/article/4702-australia-and-the-asian-ascendancy-why-upskilling-is-not-necessary-to-reap-the-rewards.

Hiroki, K. and Loveday, L. (1998) The Japanese immigrant community in Brazil: Language contact and shift. *Journal of Multilingual and Multicultural Development* 9 (5), 423–435.

Immigration Museum (2011) History of immigration from Japan, from http://museumvictoria.com.au/origins/history.aspx?pid=33.

Janks, H. (2000) Domination, access, diversity and design: a synthesis for critical literacy education. *Educational Review* 52, 175–186.

Jansen, M. (2000) *The Making of Modern Japan*. Cambridge, MA: Harvard University Press.

Jayasuriya, L. (2006) The Australian–Asian connection: From Alfred Deakin to John Howard. Australian National University, from https://digitalcollections.anu.edu.au/handle/1885/43268.

Jukes, G. (2002) *The Russo-Japanese War 1904–1905*. Oxford: Osprey.

Jupp, J. (2007) *From White Australia to Woomera: The Story of Australian Immigration* (2nd edn). Melbourne: Cambridge University Press.

Kent, B., Pesman, R. and Troup, C. (2010) *Australians in Italy*. Melbourne: Monash University Press.

Khoo, S-E. and Lucas, D. (2004) *Australians' Ancestries, 2001* (Australian Bureau of Statistics, Australian Census Analytic Program Research Paper 2054.0, Corrigendum Issue 24 May), from http://www.ausstats.abs.gov.au/ausstats/free.nsf/0/3382D783B76B605BCA256E91007AB88E/$File/20540_2001.pdf.

Koleth, E. (2010) *Multiculturalism: A Review of Australian Policy Statements and Recent Debates in Australia and Overseas* (Research Paper 6, 2010–11, 8 October).Australian Parliamentary Library, from http://parlinfo.aph.gov.au/parlInfo/search/display/display.w3p;query=Id:%22library/prspub/272429%22.

Lane, B. (2011) Plan unable to save study of Indonesian, *The Australian*, 16 February, from http://www.theaustralian.com.au/higher-education/plan-unable-to-save-study-of-indonesian/story-e6frgcjx-1226006527311.

Lane, B. (2013a) Talk of Asian century just that as language funding falls short, *The Australian*, 17 April, from http://www.theaustralian.com.au/higher-education/talk-of-asian-century-just-that-as-language-funding-falls-short/story-e6frgcjx-1226621969274.

Lane, B. (2013b) Labor's Asian language vision a delusion, says Stephen FitzGerald, *The Australian*, 20 February, from http://www.theaustralian.com.au/higher- education/labors-asian-language-vision-a-delusion-says-stephen-fitzgerald/story-e6frgcjx-1226581519177.

Liddicoat, A.J. and Scarino, A. (eds) (2010) *Languages in Australian Education: Problems, Prospects and Future Directions*. Newcastle: Cambridge Scholars Publishing.

Lo Bianco, J. (1987) *National Policy on Languages*. Canberra: Australian Government Publishing Service.

Lo Bianco, J. (1999) Policy words: Talking bilingual education and ESL into English literacy. *Prospect* 14 (2), 40–52.

Lo Bianco, J. (2001) From policy to anti-policy: How fear of language rights took policy making out of community hands. In J. Lo Bianco and R. Wickert (eds) *Australian*

Policy Activism in Language and Literacy (pp. 13–44). Melbourne: Language Australia Publications.

Lo Bianco, J. (2003) Language education in Australia: Italian and Japanese as symbols of culture policy. In J. Bourne and E. Reid (eds) *World Yearbook of Education 2003* (pp. 171–188). London: Kogan Page.

Lo Bianco, J. (2004) Language planning as applied linguistics. In A. Davies and C. Elder (eds) *The Handbook of Applied Linguistics* (pp. 738–763). London: Blackwell.

Lo Bianco, J. (2005) *Asian Languages in Australian Schools: Policy Options.* (Melbourne Asia Policy Papers, No. 7, May). Melbourne: Melbourne Institute of Asian Languages and Societies.

Lo Bianco, J. (2007) Our (not so) polyglot pollies. *Australian Review of Applied Linguistics* 30(2), 1–21.

Lo Bianco, J. (2008) Tense times and language policy. *Current Issues in Language Planning* 9 (2), 155–178.

Lo Bianco, J. (2009) Return of the good times? Japanese teaching today. *Japanese Studies* 29 (3), 331–336.

Lo Bianco, J. (2010a) The importance of language policies and multilingualism for cultural diversity. *International Social Science Journal* 61, 37–67.

Lo Bianco, J. (2010b) Language policy and planning. In N.H. Hornberger and S.L. McKay (eds) *Sociolinguistics and Language Education* (pp. 143–176). Bristol: Multilingual Matters.

Lo Bianco, J. and Gvozdenko, I. (2006) *Collaboration and Innovation in the Provision of Languages Other Than English in Australian Universities.* Melbourne: Faculty of Education, University of Melbourne, from http://www.lcnau.org/pdfs/LO%20BIANCO%20GVOZDENKO%20LOTES%20in%20Australian%20Universities.pdf.

Lo Bianco, J. and Slaughter, Y. (2009) *Second Languages and Australian Schooling: Review and Proposals* (Australian Education Review 54). Camberwell: Australian Council for Education Research.

Lo Bianco, J., Orton, J. and Gao, Y. (eds) (2009) *China and English: Globalisation and Dilemmas of Identity.* Bristol: Multilingual Matters.

Machiavelli, N. (1515) *The Prince* (W.K. Marriott, trans., 1908), from http://www.constitution.org/mac/prince06.htm.

Macklin, J. and Garrett, P. (2009) *Indigenous Languages – A National Approach. The Importance of Australia's Indigenous Languages.* Canberra: Australian Government Department of Environment, Water, Heritage and the Arts.

Maidment, R. and Mackerras, C. (1998) *Culture and Society in the Asia–Pacific.* London: Routledge.

Martin, S. (1998) The AMEP: A 50-year contribution to the development of a multicultural nation. *Prospect* 13 (3), 11.

Masterson, D. and Funada-Classen, S. (2004) *The Japanese in Latin America: The Asian American Experience.* Urbana, IL: University of Illinois Press.

McGregor, J. (2011) Australian students in the dark as Asia's century dawns. *The Age,* 13 April, from http://www.theage.com.au/opinion/society-and-culture/australian-students-in-the-dark-as-asias-century-dawns-20110412-1dcje.html.

McKeown, B. and Thomas, D. (1988) *Q Methodology.* Newbury Park, CA: Sage Publications.

Ministerial Council for Education, Employment, Training and Youth Affairs (2005) *National Statement for Languages Education in Australian Schools 2005–2008; National Plan for Languages Education in Australian Schools.* Hindmarsh: Department of

Education and Children's Services, State of South Australia, from http://www. mceetya.edu.au/verve/_resources/languageeducation_file.pdf.

Moss, D. (2004) Anomalies in the academy: The vicissitudes of Italian studies in Australia. *Arts and Humanities in Higher Education* 3 (2), 125–146.

Nichols, P. (1973) *Italia, Italia*. London: Macmillan.

Oliver, P. (2001) Japanese under white Australian. In J. Jupp (ed.) *The Australian People: An Encyclopedia of the Nation, Its People and Their Origins* (pp. 523–524). Cambridge: Cambridge University Press.

Ostler, N. (2005) *Empires of the Word: A Language History of the World*. London: Harper Collins.

Ostler, N. (2007) *Ad Infinitum: A Biography of Latin*. London: Harper Collins.

Ostler, N. (2010) *The Last Lingua Franca: English Until the Return of Babel*. London: Allen Lane Penguin.

Price, C. (1998) Post-war immigration: 1945–1998. *Journal of Population Research* 15 (2), 115–129.

Price, C. and Hugo, G. (2000) *Immigration, Settlement and Ethnicity in Postwar Australia: A Selection of the Writings of Charles A. Price* (G. Hugo, ed.). Adelaide: Australian Population Association.

Price, S. (2011) Let's ditch the study of languages. *Herald Sun*, 3 February, from http://www.heraldsun.com.au/opinion/lets-ditch-the-study-of-languages/story-e6frfhqf-1225999139631.

Roberts, A. (2006) *A History of the English-Speaking Peoples Since 1900*. London: Weidenfeld and Nicolson.

Roskam, J. (2008) 2020 summit 'a PR stunt', ABC News, from http://www.abc.net.au/news/2008-04-21/2020-summit-a-pr-stunt/2410670.

Rudd, K. (1995) Creating an Asia-literate Australia. In G. Sheridan (ed.) *Living with Dragons: Australia Confronts Its Destiny*. St Leonards: Allen and Unwin/Mobil Oil.

Sheridan, G. (2011) Neighbourhood botch. *The Australian*, 4 June, from http://www.theaustralian.com.au/news/arts/neighbourhood-botch/story-e6frg8nf-12260 67039028.

Simpson, J., Caffery, J. and McConvell, P. (2009) *Gaps in Australia's Indigenous Language Policy: Dismantling Bilingual Education in the Northern Territory* (Discussion Paper 24). Canberra: Australian Institute of Aboriginal and Torres Strait Islander Studies.

Sissons, D. (2001) Japanese. In J. Jupp (ed.) *The Australian People: An Encyclopaedia of the Nation, Its People and Their Origins* (pp. 522–524). Cambridge: Cambridge University Press.

Slattery, L. (2007) A blinkered approach to languages. *The Australian*, 7 November, from http://www.theaustralian.com.au/higher-education/opinion-analysis/a-blinkered-approach-to-languages/story-e6frgclx-1111114814855.

Sori, E. (1979) *L'emigrazione italiana dall'Unità alla seconda guerra mondiale*. Bologna: Il Mulino.

State of Victoria (2009) *Education for Global and Multicultural Citizenship: A Strategy for Victorian Government Schools 2009–2013*. Melbourne: Office of Government School Education, DEECD.

Stephenson, W. (1953) *The Study of Behavior: Q-Technique and Its Methodology*. Chicago, IL: University of Chicago Press.

Sturak, K. and Naughten, Z. (2010) *The Current State of Chinese, Indonesian, Japanese and Korean Language Education in Australian Schools* (electronic resource: four languages, four stories). Carlton South: Asia Education Foundation, from http://foi.deewr.gov.au/node/26152.

Tollefson, J. (2002) Conclusion: looking outward. In J. Tollefson (ed.) *Language Policies in Education* (pp. 327–339). Mahwah, NJ: Erlbaum.

Tomazin, F. (2009) $11b plan to teach Asian languages. *The Age*, 10 June, from http://www.theage.com.au/national/education/11bn-plan-to-teach-asian-languages-20090609-c28l.html.

Totaro-Genevois, M. (2005) *Cultural and Linguistic Policy Abroad: The Italian Experience*. Clevedon: Multilingual Matters.

Tsuda, T. (2003) *Strangers in the Ethnic Homeland: Japanese Brazilian Return Migration in Transnational Perspective*. Cambridge: Cambridge University Press.

VCAA (Victorian Curriculum and Assessment Authority) (2007) *Victorian Essential Learning Standards*. Melbourne: VCAA.

Victorian Department of Education and Training (2002) *Languages for Victoria's Future: An Analysis of Languages in Government Schools*. Melbourne: Victorian Department of Education and Training.

Ward, L. (2007) Never mind French and Spanish.... *Education Guardian*, 4 February, from http://www.guardian.co.uk/education/2007/apr/02/schools.uk.

Watson-Gegeo, K. (2004) Mind, language, and epistemology: Toward a language socialization paradigm for SLA. *Modern Language Journal* 88 (3), 331–350.

Watts, S. and Stenner, P. (2012) *Doing Q-Methodological Research: Theory, Method and Interpretation*. London: Sage.

Index